Taste of Eastern India

Delicious, Authentic Bengali Meals You Need to Try

Kankana Saxena
Creator of Playful Cooking

PAGE STREET
PUBLISHING CO.

PAGE STREET
PUBLISHING CO.

First published in 2018 by

Page Street Publishing Co.

27 Congress Street, Suite 105

Salem, MA 01970

www.pagestreetpublishing.com

Distributed by Macmillan, sales in Canada by The Canadian Manda Group.

22   21   20   19   18   1   2   3   4   5

ISBN-13: 978-1-62414-603-9

ISBN-10: 1-62414-603-1

Library of Congress Control Number: 2018933906

Cover and book design by Rosie Gutmann for Page Street Publishing Co.

Photography by Kankana Saxena

Printed and bound in China

Page Street Publishing protects our planet by donating to nonprofits like The Trustees, which focuses on local land conservation.

Table of Contents

Introduction

My love for food didn't start at an early age. I was picky and a very slow eater. Mealtime was boring for me and I never looked forward to it. Occasionally, my younger brother used to prepare snacks and breakfast for us. However, I never had the interest to even enter the kitchen. The very first time I cooked a dish was when I was probably in 8th grade. Ma was not well, Baba was traveling for work and my brother had an exam. So, I had to help Ma in whatever way I could to put a meal together for us three. She never approved of eating out, and homemade food was always the route. I remember making a very simple mixed vegetable stew. Ma was guiding me through the steps and I followed them to the letter. To my surprise, it turned out quite tasty and even my brother, who is a very tough critic, went for a second serving. Even though I was very happy and motivated to cook more, it took me many more years to actually enter the kitchen with a happy heart.

When I left home and started to live on my own in a different city, the biggest challenge, as expected, was making a decent meal. Most often, I would go for takeout or survive on instant noodles or toast with an egg. Food for me was just fuel to survive, and I would eat it without really enjoying it.

Then came a time in my life when I started to travel across the globe for work. Visiting those different places, meeting new people, eating together with them and sharing stories did some kind of magic to my appetite. Whenever my brother would call me and ask about my trip, the first thing I used to talk about was the food that I tried and liked. My brother's reply used to be, "You are talking about food!" Slowly, I started to make more visits to the grocery store and try my hand with these dishes. Eventually, I realized that cooking helped me release all the stress. I started to enjoy my time in the kitchen, and the entire process made me happier.

When I moved to the United States after marrying my boyfriend of four years, I had to leave my job and get on a visa that didn't allow me to work. For the first two months, I loved the break—no morning rush, no deliverables and no meetings. I spent a lot of time binge-watching some good old TV shows. Then, one afternoon after a long chat with my friend Deepa, I decided to start a food blog. I seriously had no idea about this blogging world, but I figured it would be a nice way to use those ample free hours that I had in hand. Arvind, my husband, helped me with all the technical stuff and we came up with a blog called Sunshine and Smile. After a few years, the name started to bother me, so I changed it to Playful Cooking. It became my culinary playground where I shared my love for food, photography and memories made at every meal!

In my blog, I share different kinds of dishes because that's how we eat on a daily basis. Arvind is not Bengali. He is from northern India, and coming from two different food cultures has made our day-to-day meals quite an interesting blend of cuisines.

While writing this book, I wanted to go back to my roots and bring more awareness to Bengali cuisine. It's much more than just *roshogolla* and *macher jhol*! This book is not an extension of my blog. It's a different journey altogether, where I turned my multi-cuisine kitchen into a Bengali kitchen and went back to my roots.

A Little Bit about Bengali Culture and Food

Known for their love of food, music and literature, the Bengali population lives mainly in the northeastern part of the South Asian subcontinent. But regardless of which part of the world they live in, they like to carry on with their traditions and culture, their festivals and celebrations. It's a vital part of life for Bengalis all over the world.

I was born and brought up in a small hill station, Shillong, in northeastern India. Both my parents are Bengalis and I grew up following the authentic Bengali tradition: listening to *Rabindra Sangeet* (songs written and composed by the late poet Rabindranath Tagore) and even trying to learn them as a kid, and watching Ma drape a crisp cotton saree effortlessly every single day, which for me is the most beautiful attire.

I especially love the white saree with the vibrant red border that is typically worn on any festive occasion and is the pride of Bengali culture.

Bengalis' love for food is legendary. I grew up in a family where everybody loves food, everybody knows how to cook and when we all get together, there is always a lot to eat. Whether it's a weekday or a weekend or a celebration of a festival, an array of dishes is prepared and served in sequential order. That's the Bengali way of eating! An everyday menu always includes a lentil stew with some fried vegetables or fried fish, followed by a vegetarian dish. Then comes the nonvegetarian curry, mostly fish, and on weekends, poultry or meat. In summer, the meal ends with a tangy stew or sweet-spicy chutney. But if it's a special occasion, after the chutney, there is a sweet treat. Dig deep and you will realize that it's a well-balanced meal incorporating every single flavor from bitter to spicy to sour to sweet.

Bengali meals are served in either brass or stainless steel plates and bowls. Rice is served with ghee on the plate along with lemon wedges and a pinch of salt. The rest of the items are served in tiny bowls following the pattern of lighter to richer. These bowls are placed in order around the plate, making it extremely visually appealing. Forks and knives are never involved; instead, food is eaten with clean hands. We like to embrace the texture of the food with our fingers before putting it in our mouth. This eating habit is not considered unhealthy, but is said to stimulate your digestive juices.

About This Book

Bengali cooking is often symbolized by the pungent aroma of smoky mustard oil followed by the nutty whiff of *paanch phoron*, a traditional spice blend, crackling in the hot oil. Most often that is the only flavor component used in a dish. Bengali cooking doesn't always involve a lot of spices, as most of the dishes have subtle flavor with a hint of heat from fresh green chillies. Chilli powder is very rarely used. Even the Bengali *gorom moshla* is quite smooth in flavor, prepared with just three whole spices. The dishes are often slow cooked to create a delicate taste. Baking and roasting are not practiced. Rice is the primary staple, and freshwater fish is the dominant kind of protein used in everyday meals. Although mustard oil is the primary choice for cooking oil, these days this pungent oil is being restricted to certain rich dishes only. Instead, vegetable oil, referred to as *shada tel* (white oil), is being used for regular cooking.

The various traders and invaders who have made Bengal their home in the past had a huge influence on the food culture. These influences made the flavor of Bengali cuisine unique and vibrant, yet it's still simple cooking with everyday ingredients.

In this book, throughout the different chapters, I share some of the dishes that I grew up eating, ranging from comfort food to street food. Every family has its own version of these dishes, and I share what I learned from my Ma. We grew up eating seasonal food. Even today, Baba will stop by at the market every other day and bring home a bag full of fresh vegetables and freshwater fish. Chicken and mutton are left for weekends, and again these are always purchased fresh in the morning. Even today, my parents follow the same ritual.

I have stayed true to the authenticity of the cuisine. The chapters are aligned as per the courses served. The meal often starts with hearty lentils or a simple veggie mash paired with some deep-fried fritters. Then comes the pure vegetarian main dishes, followed by a meat, fish or egg main dish, which is then followed by something tangy or a sweet chutney. On weekends or special occasions, the meal always ends with dessert. In the last chapter, I took a detour from the authenticity and gave a fun little twist to some of the Bengali dishes, so that chapter is a blend of sweet and savory appetizers and mains.

None of the dishes are extremely difficult to prepare. I added notes, tips and any kind of alternative that might be applicable. If you have your pantry stocked with the commonly used spice mixes, getting a Bengali meal ready won't be any hassle.

Through this book, I hope to bring out the essences of Bengal. I hope these dishes will inspire you to cook and that you will enjoy it as much as I do.

Let's Start with the Basics

Cooking Bengali food is as easy as it gets. At the end of the book (page 184), you will find a list of spices that are commonly used in Bengali cuisine. Some of those spices are then mixed together to create spice blends that are unique to Bengali dishes. I recommend preparing these spice blends in small quantities for the freshest flavor.

In addition to the spice blends, in this chapter I include a basic recipe for *bhaat* (steamed white rice), *ruti* (whole wheat Indian flatbread), *luchi* (deep-fried puffed mini bread) and *chaana* (fresh unripened cheese).

Spice Blends

Bengali Gorom Moshla

20 green cardamom pods

2-inch (5-cm) cinnamon stick

1 tbsp (11 g) cloves

Dry roast the spices in a hot pan for a few seconds, and then grind to a powder in a clean coffee grinder dedicated to spices or in a mortar and pestle. Store in an airtight jar. (Photo upper right)

Bhaja Moshla

Dry roast equal portions of cumin seeds, coriander seeds and fennel seeds in a hot pan for a few seconds. Grind them to a coarse texture in a clean coffee grinder dedicated to spices or in a mortar and pestle. Store in an airtight jar. (Photo upper left)

Paanch Phoron

Mix equal portions of nigella seeds, cumin seeds, black mustard seeds, fennel seeds and fenugreek seeds. Store in an airtight jar. (Photo lower left)

Shorshe Baata

Soak yellow mustard seeds in water for a few hours to soften, and then grind to a smooth paste along with a few green chillies and a pinch of salt in a blender or in a mortar and pestle.

The tricky thing about this spice paste is that if you grind mustard seeds for too long, they will turn bitter and inedible, so you need to soak the seeds to soften them to make grinding easier. I prefer to grind this in a mortar and pestle instead of a blender. But, if you have to use a blender, just make sure you don't run the blender for too long.

These days, you can get dry mustard powder in the market and all you have to do is mix water with it. You could also grind dry mustard seeds using a coffee or spice grinder and then store the powder in an airtight container for months. When you need to make the paste, just mix water with the ground mustard seeds along with finely chopped green chillies and salt, and pound to form a smooth paste. (Photo lower right)

Posto Baata

Soak poppy seeds in water for a few hours to soften, and then grind to a smooth paste along with a few green chillies in a blender or in a mortar and pestle. As with *shorshe baata*, I find it easier to grind this using a mortar and pestle, unless I have to make a big batch, in which case I use a blender.

Bhaat

(Steamed White Rice)

Serves 2

Bhaat to Bengalis is not just a daily food but is also very sacred. There are several ceremonies dedicated to the beauty of consuming rice. *Mukhe Bhaat/Annaprashan* is the first big festival in a child's life and happens when they are six months old and they taste rice for the first time. *Aiburo Bhaat* is another family festival where a soon-to-be-married bride and groom are given a feast that includes their favorite dishes. Then comes *Bou Bhaat*, when a newly-wed bride enters the kitchen for the first time and prepares rice for the family.

1 cup (211 g) short-grain white rice

1½ cups (355 ml) water

Rinse the rice in several changes of water and then let it soak in a bowl of water for about 30 minutes. Soaking the rice makes it fluffy and also speeds the cooking process.

Place a heavy-bottomed pan over medium-high heat and pour in the water. Once the water comes to a boil, drain the soaked rice and very carefully add it into the boiling water. Stir and let the water come to a boil once again. Then lower the heat to medium and let the rice simmer for 15 minutes, or until the water is absorbed and the rice is almost cooked. Turn off the heat and cover the pan for 5 minutes. Fluff using a fork and it's ready to eat.

Chaana

(Fresh Unripened Cheese)

Makes 1½ cups (344 g)

Chaana is a fresh, unripened cheese that is prepared by curdling whole milk with something acidic, like lemon juice or vinegar. It's a very fast process and the cheese turns out moist. Chaana plays a very important role in Bengali diet. A wide variety of desserts and savory dishes are prepared with it. Growing up, I didn't like drinking milk, so occasionally Ma would give me a break from milk and prepare fresh chaana. Sprinkle some sugar on top and it becomes a healthy, protein-packed snack. In the Sweet Tooth chapter (page 129), you will find several sweet treats prepared using chaana and in the Plant-Based Main Dishes chapter (page 73) you will find a savory, hearty recipe prepared with the fresh cheese.

Key Notes: Cooling the milk slightly before curdling makes the texture of the chaana soft. It is important not to let the curdled milk hang in a cheesecloth for more than 40 minutes or the moisture gets completely drained out. If it completely dries out, it will spoil the final texture of the dishes that you will prepare with it. Any recipe that calls for chaana cannot be replaced with store-bought *paneer* because the texture of fresh chaana is very different.

3 tbsp (44 ml) white vinegar or lemon juice

3 tbsp (44 ml) water

3 ice cubes

4 cups (946 ml) whole milk

Line a colander with a cheesecloth folded in half and place the colander in a clean sink.

In a cup, mix the vinegar with the water and set aside. Place the ice cubes in a bowl and set aside.

Pour the milk into a heavy-bottomed saucepan and place it over medium-high heat. Stir occasionally using a wooden spoon as the milk comes to a boil.

Once the milk comes to a complete boil, turn off the heat and immediately add the ice cubes. Now pour in the water-vinegar mixture and stir. You will notice the milk start to curdle and the water will turn pale green. Carefully pour the curdled milk into the cheesecloth.

Run cold water over the collected curdled milk in the cheesecloth. This will remove the acidity from the cheese and will also cool it down.

Next, gather the edges of the cheesecloth and squeeze out as much water as possible. Then tie the corners into a knot and hang it over the sink for 30 minutes to drain out the water.

After 30 minutes, carefully untie the knot and scrape the cheese out of the cloth and into a bowl. You can sprinkle some sugar on it and enjoy right away with some fruits on the side.

Ruti

(Whole Wheat Indian Flatbread)

Makes 10

Bengalis love rice, but if rice is not an option, then it's *ruti* with some leftover curry from last night or a quick veggie stir-fry. These days, considering the fact that ruti *is* healthier than *bhaat*, Bengalis have started to add more ruti to their everyday diets.

Key Notes: Making ruti sounds very easy, but it will take some practice to get the perfect soft texture. Ruti tastes best when you eat it with your hands. You tear a tiny bite-size portion, and scoop a little bit of the stew onto it and put the entire thing in your mouth. It's casual and comfortable. Of course you can always use the same ruti as a wrap too!

2 cups (260 g) durum wheat atta or whole wheat flour

1 tsp salt

1 cup (237 ml) warm water

½ tsp oil

In a large bowl, combine the flour and salt and stir with your hand. Then pour the water little by little as you start kneading the dough. Knead the dough until it comes together into a soft dough. Then pour in the oil and knead it one last time.

Cover the dough for 15 minutes before you start making the ruti.

To prepare the ruti, divide the dough into 10 equal portions. Shape each portion into a disk. Cover the disks with a kitchen towel to keep them from drying out.

Place a skillet over medium-high heat. As the pan heats up, place one disk on the kitchen counter or chopping board, sprinkle with some flour and roll it into a 6- or 7-inch (15- or 18-cm) diameter circle.

Place the rolled dough on the hot skillet. In a few seconds, you will see bubbles appearing. Flip it carefully and let it cook for a few seconds on the other side.

The next step, where you puff the ruti, can be done in several different ways.

Option 1: Use a soft kitchen towel to press on the hot ruti gently while it's on the hot skillet. It will start puffing, and the air will start filling up. Keep pressing gently around to make the entire ruti puff up. Transfer to a plate. Prepare rest of the ruti the same way.

Option 2: Turn down the heat to medium-low and, using tongs, lift the ruti from the hot skillet, remove the skillet and hold the ruti over the open flame. It will start filling with air almost immediately. Place the puffed ruti on a plate. Prepare the rest of the ruti the same way. You have to be very careful if you follow this step. The heat of the stove should be medium-low or else the ruti will be charred a little too much.

Option 3: This is the step I follow, where I use a steel wire roaster to puff the ruti over an open flame. Using tongs, lift the ruti, remove the skillet, place the steel wire roaster over an open flame and place the ruti on it. The ruti will start to puff in seconds. Transfer to a plate. Prepare the rest of the ruti the same way.

Luchi

(Deep-Fried Puffed Mini Bread)

Makes 20

Deep-fried, airy, unleavened mini bread, *luchi* is a favorite for weekend breakfasts. Sometimes served with veggie stew and sometimes with meat, these puffed-up breads are one of my guilty pleasures. Unlike North Indian *poori*, luchi is prepared with all-purpose flour. Although it sounds like one of those simple recipes, mastering the perfect puffed luchi takes some practice.

Key Notes: Typically, luchi is prepared with only all-purpose flour, but I like to add a small amount of whole wheat flour to the mixture. It doesn't change the flavor but it makes it easier to roll out the dough.

1½ cups (149 g) all-purpose flour

¼ cup (33 g) whole wheat flour

½ tsp sugar

½ tsp salt

3 tbsp (45 ml) vegetable oil

⅔ cup (158 ml) warm water

Oil, for deep-frying

In a mixing bowl, combine the flours, sugar and salt. Stir.

Pour in the vegetable oil and mix it around nicely. When you hold a fistful of flour, it should retain its shape. If it doesn't, pour in a little more oil.

Then pour in the water and start kneading. You have to knead for about 7 to 10 minutes to form a smooth dough. Cover the dough with a kitchen towel and let it rest for 10 minutes.

After 10 minutes, knead the dough again and divide it into 20 portions. Shape each portion into a tiny disk and cover the disks with a kitchen towel.

To roll the disks, rub some oil on the disk and roll it from the center outward. Keep rotating and rolling the disk until it is a thin 4-inch (10-cm) diameter circle. The dough will be elastic and will shrink back as you roll, so put gentle pressure as you rotate and roll. Cover the rolled luchi with a kitchen towel and roll the rest of the disks.

After rolling all the disks, place a heavy-bottomed pan over medium-high heat and pour in enough oil to reach a depth of 2½ inches (6 cm).

Layer a kitchen towel on a plate and keep it ready for the hot luchi to drain excess oil.

Once the oil is between 325°F and 350°F (163°C and 177°C), very carefully slide one disk into the hot oil. Use a slotted spoon and gently press the disk on top. This technique will puff the luchi in a few seconds. Flip the luchi and fry for a few more seconds. Remove it from the hot oil to the prepared plate. Continue frying the rest of the luchi in the same manner. Serve warm.

For the Love of Rice

The presence of rice in Bengali meals is essential. It's a staple. "*Bhaat chara chole nah,*" a typical expression used often, means, "It's impossible without rice." Everyday lunch and dinner always includes *bhaat* (steamed short-grain white rice) paired with several side dishes. Somehow, most Bengali dishes are such that it tastes best with rice.

The simple rice gets elevated in different ways based on occasion. During festive seasons and on weekends, Bengali *basanti pulao* (sweet saffron pilaf) is served with a spicy mutton stew. Hearty *khichuri* (rice and lentil porridge) is a ritual for rainy days.

Then, there is *biryani* for those lazy Sundays, which gets heavily loaded with spices when prepared with meat and kept subtle when prepared with fish. There has to be *muri ghonto* (fried fish head and rice pilaf), which may sound bizarre to some, but for us Bengalis it's a delicacy.

Rice is not just a staple grain; it is also quite auspicious to us. Babies are introduced to their first solid food at six months. It's quite a ceremony. Called *Annaprashan* or *Mukhe Bhaat*, it literally translates to "rice in your mouth." The first thing that the babies taste is *khejur gur chaal er payesh* (date molasses rice pudding) and the ritual of preparing *payesh* continues with every birthday. You will find all these recipes in this chapter.

Bengali Basanti Pulao

(Sweet Saffron Pilaf)

Serves 2

Bengali basanti pulao, also known as *mishti pulao* (sweet saffron pilaf), is a quintessential rice dish prepared during every celebration and festive season. Bengalis love their rice, be it for lunch or dinner. On special occasions, the everyday steamed white rice gets uplifted with whole spices, nuts, raisins and a hint of exotic saffron. It's one of those dishes where aromatic *gobindo bhog* rice is typically used, but it can be easily replaced with any short-grain white rice.

½ tsp saffron thread

3 tbsp (44 ml) milk

1 cup (211 g) gobindo bhog or any short-grain rice

2 tbsp (29 g) ghee

1 cinnamon stick

2 bay leaves

3 green cardamom pods

5 cloves

¼ cup (38 g) raisins

¼ cup (28 g) cashews, plus more for garnish

1 tsp salt

2¼ cups (532 ml) water, divided

1 tbsp (12 g) sugar

Place the saffron in a bowl and pour in the milk. Whisk and set aside for 10 minutes. The milk will infuse and turn a saffron color.

Pour the rice into a mixing bowl and wash the rice several times in running water. Then drain using a colander and leave it there for the water to drain out completely.

Place a heavy-bottomed skillet over medium heat and add in the ghee. Once the ghee heats up, add the cinnamon, bay leaves, cardamom and cloves. Allow them to sizzle for a few seconds.

Add the raisins and cashews and toss for a few seconds or until the cashews are mildly toasted.

Next, add in the rice, sprinkle with the salt and give it a stir. Then pour the saffron milk and 2 cups (473 ml) of the water into the pan. Stir. Turn the heat down to medium and let it simmer for 15 minutes.

After 15 minutes, when the rice is almost cooked, sprinkle with the sugar and stir.

If the water is almost absorbed, pour in the remaining ¼ cup (59 ml) of water. Continue cooking for 5 more minutes.

Once the rice is cooked and the water is absorbed completely, leave the pan covered for 5 minutes and then fluff it using a fork.

Serve warm with a few more roasted cashews on top as garnish.

Bhoger Khichuri

(Roasted Yellow Split Mung Beans and Rice Porridge)

Serves 2

Bhog is a term used for a cooked pure vegetarian meal that is offered to gods and goddesses on festivals. *Khichuri* is a creamy porridge of rice and lentils, and when it's offered to gods or goddesses, it is referred to as *bhoger khichuri*. Bengalis are known for their love of nonvegetarian meals, but this warm comforting porridge wins everyone's heart. Khichuri can be prepared with any kind of lentils, but Ma always prepares it with roasted yellow split mung beans. Roasting these petite, yellow split mung beans brings out a lovely, nutty aroma and an earthy taste to the khichuri.

Key Notes: Just like risotto or rice pudding, bhoger khichuri can also thicken up as it sits. You can make the khichuri in advance, but in that case, leave it runny with more water and don't temper it. Just before serving, warm it up and then add the temper for the earthy aroma.

½ cup (100 g) yellow split mung beans

½ cup (105 g) short-grain rice

4 cups (946 ml) water

1 tsp salt

½ tsp ground turmeric

2 green chillies, sliced in half

2 tbsp (29 g) ghee

2 bay leaves

2 dried red chillies

1 tbsp (8 g) finely chopped ginger

1 tsp paanch phoron (page 11)

Lime wedges

Place a wok or a skillet over medium heat and dry roast the mung beans to a mild darker shade for about 3 minutes, stirring every now and then. Then soak the roasted beans in water to cover for 30 minutes.

Wash the rice in a colander under running water, scrubbing the rice with your hands for a few seconds. Let the rice sit in the colander to drain.

After 30 minutes, add the washed rice into a large, heavy-bottomed saucepan. Add the drained beans to the pan. Add the water, salt and turmeric. Give it a stir and place the pan over high heat.

Once the water comes to a boil, turn the heat down to medium-low and cook for about 20 minutes or until the rice and beans are almost cooked and softened. Add the green chillies and stir. If the water gets absorbed completely, pour in some more water and cook for 10 more minutes or until the consistency looks like a creamy porridge. Check for salt and add any if required. Turn off the heat once done.

Now place another small saucepan over medium-high heat. Pour in the ghee and when it starts to heat up, add the bay leaves, red chillies, ginger and *paanch phoron*. Allow the spices to sizzle for a few seconds and then pour it over the khichuri. Stir, squeeze on some fresh lime juice and serve warm.

Khejur Gur Chaal Er Payesh

(Date Molasses Rice Pudding)

Serves 4

Just as cake is a ritual on birthdays, we Bengalis also have another mandatory dessert for that special day—*payesh*! Payesh is a creamy rice pudding typically prepared with the aromatic short-grain rice called *gobindo bhog chaal*. However, it can be replaced with any short-grain rice you have on hand. It is typically sweetened with sugar but on special occasions and especially during winter, when *khejur gur* (date molasses) is in abundance, *chaal er payesh* gets uplifted with the enticing aroma and gorgeous amber shade of the date molasses.

Key Notes: If you can't find khejur gur, also referred to as *patali gur*, use any other variety of jaggery or brown sugar as a sweetener. Keep in mind that the taste of the pudding will depend on the kind of sweetener you are using.

1 cup (211 g) gobindo bhog chaal or short-grain rice

2 tbsp (19 g) raisins

2 cups (473 ml) whole milk

3 cups (710 ml) heavy cream

1 dried bay leaf

½ cup (118 ml) khejur gur (date molasses)

4 green cardamom pods, roughly crushed

2 tbsp (14 g) cashews

Using a colander, wash the rice in several changes of water and then soak it in water to cover for about 30 minutes.

In another small bowl, soak the raisins in water to cover.

In a heavy-bottomed pan, add the milk and heavy cream. Add the bay leaf and bring the milk to a boil, stirring often. Now, let it simmer over medium-low heat for about 15 minutes or until the milk thickens a bit.

Drain the rice from the water and pour it into the saucepan. Continue cooking over medium-low heat, stirring occasionally.

After about 10 minutes or so, the rice should be half cooked. Add the molasses and green cardamom and continue cooking, stirring occasionally. Once the rice is softened, add the cashews. Drain the raisins and add them to the pan. Give it a stir.

The pudding is ready to serve. Keep in mind that the pudding will thicken up as it sits at room temperature. So, if you are making it in advance and not serving right away, leave the pudding a little runny by adding more milk.

Ilish Biryani

(Hilsa Fish in Flavored Rice Pilaf)

Serves 4

Most coastal regions have their own versions of fish *biryani*. Similarly, Bengalis have their own version too, and it is often prepared with hilsa fish. Unlike the chicken biryani, *ilish biryani* is subtle in flavor and not heavily spiced. Hilsa fish is an oily, aromatic, freshwater fish. To retain the flavor of the fish, this biryani is not overloaded with spice or heat. This is one of those dishes that takes time and attention, but at the end it will feel worth the effort.

Key Notes: Hilsa fish has a lot of bones, which might be challenging if you aren't used to eating this fish. You can prepare the same dish using any big fish fillet. Catfish or salmon would be a good substitute.

4 fillets hilsa fish

1 cup (211 g) basmati rice

1 red onion

Oil for deep-frying

1 tbsp (8 g) cumin seeds

2 cups (490 g) thick plain Greek yogurt

1 tbsp (10 g) garlic paste

1 tbsp (10 g) ginger paste

2 tsp (10 g) salt, divided

1 tsp chilli powder

2 tbsp (29 g) ghee

2 bay leaves

5 green cardamom pods

1 mace

1 cinnamon stick

6 cloves

1½ cups (355 ml) water

1 tbsp (15 ml) vegetable oil

2 tbsp (30 ml) milk

5 green chillies

Clean the hilsa fish fillets and set aside.

Using a colander, wash the rice in several changes of water and leave it in the colander to drain any excess water.

Peel the red onion and cut the top and bottom. Then cut the onion in half and cut each half into thin half-moon slices.

Place a deep saucepan over medium-high heat and pour in the oil. Layer a plate with a kitchen towel and set aside. Once the oil is hot, add the sliced onion and stir with a slotted spoon until the onion turns golden brown in color. It will take about 10 minutes. Once done, layer the fried onions on the kitchen towel. In a couple of minutes the fried onion should turn crispy. Remove one-third of the fried onion and crush.

Place a pan over medium-high heat, and when the pan is hot, dry roast the cumin seeds for 2 minutes, stirring constantly. Using a mortar and pestle, grind the cumin seeds.

Next, in a large mixing bowl, whisk the yogurt with the roasted ground cumin, garlic and ginger pastes, crushed fried onion, 1 teaspoon of the salt and the chilli powder. Add the hilsa fillet carefully to the mixing bowl and coat the fillet with the yogurt mixture. It will look like a lot of marinade for 4 fillets, but the yogurt mixture will be cooked to make the sauce that goes in the biryani. Cover the bowl and allow the fish to marinate for 30 minutes.

(continued)

Ilish Biryani (Continued)

After 30 minutes, start making the rice. Heat the ghee in a heavy-bottomed saucepan over medium heat and add the bay leaves, cardamom, mace, cinnamon and cloves. Allow the whole spices to sizzle for a few seconds, and then add the washed and drained rice on top. Sprinkle with the remaining 1 teaspoon of salt and stir the rice for 2 minutes. Then pour in the water, stir and bring the water to a boil. Once the water starts boiling, turn the heat down to medium and simmer for 6 to 8 minutes or until the water is absorbed and the rice is partially cooked.

As the rice cooks, place another pan over medium-high heat. Pour in the vegetable oil. Once the pan heats up, remove the fish fillets from the yogurt mixture and carefully place in the pan. Fry for 3 minutes on each side. Transfer to a separate plate. To the same pan, pour in the rest of the yogurt mixture and cook, stirring occasionally. Once the oil releases from the sides, which will happen in about 7 minutes, turn off the heat.

The next step is to layer the rice and slow cook for 20 minutes, which can be done either in the oven or on the stovetop. If you are planning to use the oven, you'll need a large ovenproof casserole dish; if you plan to use the stovetop, you'll need a heavy-bottomed saucepan with a tight-fitting lid.

Oven method: Preheat the oven to 350°F (177°C).

Brush some ghee on the bottom of the casserole dish, then layer half of the partially cooked rice, followed by half of the spiced yogurt sauce from the pan. (Don't add the fish fillet yet.) Then pour in the milk and add on half of the crispy fried onion. Next, layer the rest of the rice, the rest of the yogurt sauce and the fish fillets. Press the fish fillets down gently. Poke the green chillies all around with a sharp knife. Add them around the fish fillets. Finally, add the rest of the crispy fried onions on top.

Tightly cover the casserole dish with aluminum foil and place it on the middle rack of the oven. Bake for 20 minutes.

Stovetop method: Follow the same layering procedure as for the oven method, but in a heavy-bottomed saucepan. Place the saucepan over medium-low heat, cover the pan and allow it to slow cook for 20 minutes. Serve warm.

Kolkata Chicken Biryani

(Chicken and Potato Spiced Pilaf)

Serves 4

Biryani is a labor of love. It needs time and attention, which is why I consider it a weekend meal. When you finally open the tight lid and the aroma releases, you will find it worth all the effort.

There are numerous versions of chicken biryani found in Indian cuisine. Kolkata chicken biryani is probably the only one that has big chunks of potatoes in it. Clearly, this shows the Bengalis' love for potatoes. The story goes that several years back, when biryani was prepared for the king and his friends, the cook ran short of chicken and he added potatoes to increase the volume. Although the chef was worried, it turns out that everybody really liked the extra carb and the new twist. Since then, adding potatoes in biryani became a norm in Kolkata. Whether the story is true or not, meat and potato is always a great combination.

Key Notes: I prefer to prepare biryani with bone-in chicken pieces, because it keeps the meat moist without the risk of overcooking and drying out the chicken. However, you can always go for boneless too. If you choose boneless, then you have to be careful of the cooking time, as it will cook much faster than the time I call for in the recipe directions.

1 tbsp (10 g) cumin seeds

1 tbsp (10 g) coriander seeds

½ tsp black peppercorns

2 cinnamon sticks, divided

5 green cardamom pods, divided

3 bay leaves, divided

1 mace

1 lb (500 g) chicken pieces

1 tbsp (10 g) grated garlic

1 tbsp (8 g) grated ginger

⅓ cup (82 g) thick yogurt

1 tbsp (15 g) salt, divided

⅓ cup (79 ml) milk

½ tsp saffron threads

1 cup (211 g) long-grain basmati rice

2 red onions

Oil, for deep-frying

2 tbsp (30 ml) vegetable oil

2 medium potatoes, peeled and cut into quarters

2 tbsp (29 g) ghee, divided

4 cloves

1 star anise

1½ cups (355 ml) water

1 tbsp (15 ml) rosewater (optional)

2 hard-boiled eggs, peeled and sliced

Place a pan over medium heat and add the cumin seeds, coriander seeds, black pepper, 1 of the cinnamon sticks, 3 of the green cardamom pods, 2 of the bay leaves and the mace. Dry roast for a few seconds, and then let the spices cool for a while before grinding to a fine powder.

(continued)

Kolkata Chicken Biryani (Continued)

Place the chicken pieces in a bowl and add half of the ground spice mix, then add the garlic, ginger, yogurt and 1 teaspoon of the salt. Mix everything together and let the chicken marinate for at least 4 hours. Keeping it overnight will enhance the flavor even more.

Pour the milk into a bowl and crush the saffron threads into it. Stir and let the milk infuse for 5 minutes.

Wash the rice several times under running water. This will remove the excess starch. Then leave the washed rice in the colander for about 15 minutes for any excess water to drain out.

Peel the onions and thinly slice them. Half of the sliced onions will be deep-fried and the other half will be used in cooking the chicken.

Place a heavy-bottomed saucepan over medium heat and pour in enough oil to reach a depth of 2 inches (5 cm). Place a kitchen towel on a plate and keep it ready for the fried onions. Once the oil reaches between 325°F and 350°F (163°C and 177°C), add the sliced onion carefully and stir every now and then so the onion gets golden brown evenly. Once the onions turn light golden brown, remove from the hot oil and place on the kitchen towel.

To prepare the chicken, place another heavy-bottomed pan over medium-high heat and add in the vegetable oil. When the oil heats up, add the quartered potatoes and sprinkle with ½ teaspoon of salt. Fry for 5 minutes, tossing and turning. Transfer the potatoes to a separate bowl.

To the same pan, add the remaining sliced onion, sprinkle with ½ teaspoon of salt and cook the onion for about 4 minutes, or until softened. Then add the marinated chicken and cook for 10 minutes, tossing and turning every now and then. Turn off the heat once the chicken is partially cooked.

Place another heavy-bottomed pan over medium heat and add 1 tablespoon (15 ml) of the ghee. Once it heats up, add the remaining 1 cinnamon stick, remaining 1 bay leaf, remaining 2 cardamom pods, cloves and star anise. Allow the spices to sizzle for a while and then add the washed rice. Sprinkle with 1 teaspoon of salt and stir the rice. Let the rice roast for a couple of minutes, then pour in the water. Let the rice cook for 15 minutes or until it's half cooked.

Now finally, to prepare the biryani, preheat the oven to 350°F (177°C) and grease a large ceramic ovenproof bowl with some ghee. Layer half of the partially cooked chicken, and top it with half of the partially cooked rice. Arrange half of the fried potatoes by pushing them down a little. Add half of the fried onions evenly on top and add ½ tablespoon (7 g) of the ghee, half of the rosewater and half of the saffron milk. Repeat with the remaining chicken, rice, potato, fried onion, ghee, rosewater and saffron milk.

Cover the pan tightly with aluminum foil and bake for 20 minutes or until the rice and chicken are cooked through. Just before serving, top it with the sliced egg and enjoy while it is still warm.

Muri Ghonto

(Fish Head Rice Pilaf)

Serves 2

Eating fish head is a delicacy in Bengal and we prepare it in several different ways: as a stew, in a curry and stir-fried. One of the most common ways to prepare a large fish head is with spiced rice and then served with more white rice. That may sound weird to many, but it's a favorite to us Bengalis. Of course, you don't have to restrict yourself to that rule and can enjoy the pilaf as is with some fresh lemon juice sprinkled on top.

Key Notes: If you prefer, substitute the fish head with jumbo shrimp or chunky cauliflower nuggets.

1 potato

1 carp or rohu fish head

2 tsp (10 g) salt, divided

1 tsp ground turmeric, divided

¼ cup (59 ml) mustard oil

2 bay leaves

2 dried red chillies

1 tsp paanch phoron (page 11)

1 tsp ground cumin

1 tsp ground coriander

½ tsp chilli powder

¾ cup (158 g) short-grain rice

1¼ cups (296 ml) water

1 fresh green or red chilli, thinly sliced

1 tsp gorom moshla (page 11)

Lemon/lime wedges

Peel the potato. Slice it in half lengthwise, then slice each half into wedges and each wedge in half lengthwise. Set aside. Place the clean fish head in a big bowl and sprinkle with ½ teaspoon of the salt and ½ teaspoon of the turmeric. Massage the seasonings into the fish head and let it rest for 15 minutes.

Place a heavy-bottomed pan over medium heat and pour in the mustard oil. When the oil heats up, carefully (as it will splatter) place the fish head in the hot oil. Let it fry for 2 minutes, then flip and fry for 2 more minutes. Turn off the heat and transfer the fried fish head to a plate.

To prepare the pilaf you will need 2 tablespoons (15 ml) of the oil in the pan, so remove the rest of the oil and save it for future use or discard. Turn the heat back on to medium heat and once the oil heats up, add the potato slices. Stir and cook for 2 minutes, then transfer to a separate bowl.

To the same pan, add the bay leaves, dried red chillies and *paanch phoron* and let it sizzle for a few seconds. Then sprinkle in the remaining ½ teaspoon of turmeric, cumin, coriander and chilli powder. Stir and let the spices cook for a few seconds, then add the rice on top. Add the remaining 1½ teaspoons (8 g) of salt. Stir and let the rice sear for 2 minutes.

Add the fried potatoes, stir and then add the water. Crank up the heat and bring the water to a boil, then lower the heat to medium and cover the pan with a tight lid. Let it cook for 10 minutes, then break the fried fish head in half and layer it on the partially cooked rice. Cover the pan and let it cook for 5 more minutes. If the water gets absorbed but the rice is still uncooked, add a little bit more water and continue cooking until the rice is almost done. It shouldn't be mushy. Check for salt and add any if required. Once the rice is cooked, sprinkle with the green chilli and *gorom moshla* and stir gently. Cook for another 2 minutes. Then turn off the heat, and keep the pan covered for 5 minutes. Use a fork to fluff the rice, squeeze fresh lemon/lime juice on top and serve warm.

Deep-Fried Goodness

Bhaja, meaning "fried," is every Bengali's weak point, irrespective of the current season. Everyday meals often include at least one variety of shallow- or deep-fried food using a wide variety of seasonal vegetables and freshwater fish. They are most often sprinkled with just salt and turmeric and occasionally coated with spiced flour batter before deep-frying.

Kolkata street food is known for satiating hungry travelers with crunchy fried indulgences. It's common to come across tiny food stalls in every corner serving piping hot, crunchy, deep-fried snacks on a piece of old newspaper alongside a dollop of ketchup or *kashundi* (page 116).

When preparing these dishes, a heavy-bottomed skillet or a wok is essential. It's important to slowly heat the oil to about 350°F (177°C). If you don't have a thermometer, just dip the tip of a wooden spoon or a chopstick into the oil. If steady bubbles start appearing immediately, you know that the oil is hot enough for frying.

Beguni

(Crispy Eggplant Slices)

Makes 17

These eggplant fritters are unlike any other. Thinly sliced eggplant is dipped in a light airy batter and deep-fried to a crispy texture. As simple as it sounds, getting the consistency of the batter right is critical for it to be crunchy. This is one of the most popular street foods and is served with puffed rice and a few green chillies on the side. Other serving options include *bhoger khichuri* (roasted yellow split mung beans and rice porridge) or as a breakfast option with *luchi* (deep-fried puffed mini bread) and *cholar daal* (split Bengal gram stew).

Key Notes: The batter should be whisked for a while to make it airy and light. Don't let the batter rest for too long. Prepare the batter only when you are ready to deep-fry the eggplant slices.

1 medium Italian or classic globe eggplant (200 g/7 oz)

1 tsp sugar

1½ tsp (8 g) salt, divided

⅓ cup (50 g) rice flour

⅓ cup (42 g) all-purpose flour

½ tsp ground turmeric

1 tsp nigella seeds

¾ cup (177 ml) ice-cold water

Oil, for deep-frying

Using a sharp knife, slice the eggplant into ¼-inch (½-cm) thick circles. It should make about 17 circular slices. Place the slices in a big bowl and sprinkle with the sugar and 1 teaspoon of the salt. Massage the slices and place in a colander to rest for 30 minutes. This will soften the eggplant and release some water.

After 30 minutes, layer a plate with a kitchen towel. Place the eggplant slices on the kitchen towel. Place another kitchen towel on top and press it gently to remove the excess water that was released from the eggplant.

Now prepare the batter. In a mixing bowl, combine the rice flour, all-purpose flour, remaining ½ teaspoon of salt, turmeric and nigella seeds. Stir and pour in the ice-cold water. Now, either using a hand whisk or an electric whisk, whisk the batter to a smooth consistency. Whisk for at least 3 minutes to make the batter airy, which will ensure that the fried eggplant slices come out crispy.

Place a heavy-bottomed saucepan or wok over medium-high heat and pour in enough oil to reach a depth of 1½ inches (4 cm). When the oil reaches 350°F (177°C), whisk the batter one more time.

Keep a plate layered with a kitchen towel nearby.

Now, depending on how big your frying pan is, dunk a few slices of eggplant into the batter, allow it to coat completely and shake off any excess batter. Very carefully slide the slices into the hot oil. Fry for 3 minutes on one side, flip using tongs or a slotted spoon and fry for 2 more minutes on the other side. Remove from the pan using a slotted spoon, and place on the plate with the kitchen towel. Continue frying the rest of the eggplant slices.

Serve the crispy eggplant slices warm.

Mushuri Daal Er Boda

(Red Lentil Fritters)

Makes 15

This is the most frequently prepared fritter for a lazy afternoon lunch. It is served as the first course with warm steamed rice drizzled with ghee. Sometimes it is also served as a snack, munched with puffed rice and a hot cup of tea. Ma's favorite way to enjoy these humble fuss-free fritters is with *panta bhaat* (fermented leftover steamed white rice, page 70). Another favorite way to enjoy these fritters is with *bhaat* (steamed white rice, page 12) and *piyaj mushuri daal* (onion and red lentil soup, page 69).

½ cup (101 g) red split lentils

½ red onion

1 green chilli

1 tsp salt

1 tsp ground cumin

1 tbsp (8 g) grated ginger

Oil, for deep-frying

Soak the lentils in water to cover for about 3 hours. After 3 hours, the lentils will puff up and absorb most of the water. You can also let them soak overnight.

Chop the onion as finely as you can. Finely chop the green chilli.

When you are ready to make the fritters, transfer the lentils (don't add any water) to a clean blender or chopper and blend to a course texture. Mix in the chopped onion, green chilli, salt, cumin and ginger. Combine to mix everything.

Place a heavy-bottomed saucepan over medium-high heat and pour in oil to a depth of about 2 inches (5 cm). Layer a plate with a kitchen towel.

Once the oil heats up, using a spoon, a small cookie scooper or just by hand, add 1 tablespoon (15 g) of the batter to the hot oil. Do not overcrowd the pan. Fry the fritters for about 5 minutes, turning around every now and then, so the fritters turn an evenly golden color.

Remove the fritters from the oil with a slotted spoon and drain on the kitchen towel. Repeat with the remaining batter and serve immediately.

Posto Narkol Boda

(White Poppy Seeds and Coconut Fritters)

Makes 7

Crunchy on the outside and soft inside, these fritters are quite the favorite. They are often prepared with just white poppy seeds, but I like the addition of freshly grated coconut because it adds a subtle sweetness. The combination of spicy green chilli, earthy poppy seeds and slightly sweet coconut makes a perfect flavor balance. These are typically served with any kind of lentil stew and *bhaat* (steamed white rice, page 12), but they can easily pass as a snack as well.

Key Notes: The fritters are quite fragile and can break apart easily. So, when frying, make sure you flip them gently.

½ cup (67 g) white poppy seeds

½ cup (38 g) freshly grated coconut

2 tbsp (19 g) finely chopped red onion

1½ tbsp (14 g) rice flour

2 green chillies

¼ tsp ground turmeric

½ tsp salt

¼ cup (59 ml) water

¼ cup (59 ml) vegetable oil

Place a skillet over medium-high heat and, when hot, add the poppy seeds. Dry roast for about 30 seconds, stirring constantly. Once done, transfer to a plate and let the poppy seeds cool. Then, using a coffee/spice grinder or a mortar and pestle, grind the poppy seeds to a course texture. You could add a little water too. Transfer to a mixing bowl.

To the mixing bowl, add the rest of the ingredients except for the oil. Stir to incorporate everything into a thick, paste-like texture. Form about 2 tablespoons (20 g) of the mixture into a flat disk. Place it on a plate and continue shaping the rest of the fritters.

Place a skillet over medium heat and pour in the oil. Layer a plate with a kitchen towel. Once the oil is hot, very carefully add the fritters. Fry for 3 minutes or until the bottom is golden brown. Using a spatula, flip the patties and fry for another 3 minutes or until the bottom is golden brown.

Once done, remove the fritters from the pan to the plate with the kitchen towel. Serve warm.

Kurmure Bhendi Bhaja

(Crispy Fried Okra)

Serves 4

Okra is one of my favorite vegetables, especially when it's coated with spices and fried until crunchy. It's great as the first course of the meal paired with a light lentil stew. On Friday nights, I make a big batch and wash it down with drinks! These are typically served with any kind of lentil stew and *bhaat* (steamed white rice, page 12), but can easily pass as a snack as well.

10.5 oz (300 g) okra

½ cup (76 g) rice flour

¼ cup (44 g) fine semolina

1 tbsp (8 g) nigella seeds

½ tsp fennel seeds

1 tsp salt

½ tsp ground turmeric

½ tsp red chilli powder

1 cup (237 ml) water

Oil, for deep-frying

Wash the okra and then pat dry with a kitchen towel. Using a sharp knife, slice the okra lengthwise in half or quarters depending on their size.

In a medium-sized mixing bowl, combine the flour, semolina, nigella seeds, fennel seeds, salt, turmeric and chilli powder. Whisk to combine and then pour in the water to make a thick batter.

Add the sliced okra to the batter and toss it around to coat all the slices. Set aside for 15 minutes.

When ready to deep-fry, place a heavy-bottomed pan over medium-high heat. Pour in the oil to a depth of about 1 inch (3 cm). Have a plate layered with a kitchen towel ready.

Depending on how big your pan is, add the okra slices carefully, without overcrowding the pan. Tossing and turning, fry the okra for about 5 minutes or until golden brown in color. Remove from the pan using a slotted spoon and place on the kitchen towel to drain. The okra tastes best when served immediately.

Jhuri Aalu Bhaja

(Crispy String Potato Fries)

Serves 4

Warm lentil stew, steamed white rice, wedges of lemon and *jhuri aalu bhaja* are one of those comfort foods that we look forward to, especially on rainy days. Of course, you don't have to restrict yourself to this specific combination. These crispy, string potato fries are amazing with drinks as well.

Key Notes: You need to pay attention as you fry because these strings can go from golden brown to burned very quickly.

2 large potatoes

1½ tsp (8 g) salt

Oil, for deep-frying

¼ cup (40 g) peanuts

12 fresh mint leaves

Wash the potatoes thoroughly. Using the big holes of a cheese grater, grate the potatoes. Place the grated potatoes in a bowl and add water to cover. Sprinkle with the salt and allow the grated potatoes to soak for 15 minutes.

After 15 minutes, drain the grated potatoes using a colander. Wash the potatoes several times to get rid of as much starch as possible. Layer a kitchen towel on a plate or chopping board and spread the grated potatoes evenly on the kitchen towel. Place another towel on top and pat it lightly so the towel soaks up as much moisture as possible. Set aside for 15 minutes and allow the kitchen towel to soak up more moisture. Change the kitchen towel if needed. The grated potatoes shouldn't feel too wet.

Once you are ready to make the fries, prepare another large plate with a kitchen towel. In a deep, heavy-bottomed pan over medium-high heat, pour in enough oil to reach a depth of 1 inch (3 cm). Once the oil reaches about 350°F (177°C), add the peanuts and fry for 2 minutes. Using a slotted spoon, transfer the peanuts to the prepared plate to drain.

Next, fry the grated potatoes. Remove the kitchen towel that was on top of the layered grated potatoes. Take a handful of the grated potatoes and very carefully add it to the hot oil. Depending on how big your pan is, fry in batches without overcrowding. Adding too much will clump the potatoes. Using a slotted spoon, stir for 2 to 3 minutes, or until the potato strings look golden brown in color. Transfer to the plate with the fried peanuts. Sprinkle a pinch of salt on and continue frying the rest of the grated potatoes.

Once you are done with the potatoes, turn off the heat and add the mint leaves to the pan. They will sizzle and curl up immediately. Remove with the slotted spoon and add the leaves on top of the fried potatoes. Toss everything very delicately and serve. The potatoes stay crunchy even after several hours and can be stored in an airtight container once cooled completely.

Ilish Maach Bhaja

(Deep-Fried Hilsa Fish)

Serves 3

Maach bhaja (fish fry) is part of the daily Bengali menu and is often paired with lentil stew and steamed rice. But when hilsa fish (Ilish Maach), the most popular seasonal seafood, starts showing up in the market, *ilish maach bhaja* always takes priority. The aromatic soft fish is fried in mustard oil and savored with steamed rice along with some hot oil from the pan. Thinly sliced onion and green chillies add to the entire gastronomic experience. When I make this, I don't need any other side dish to finish my meal.

Key Notes: Use extreme caution while frying the fish fillet. Sometimes the oil can splatter a lot as you fry the fish, so keep a lid ready to cover the pan.

3 hilsa fish fillets

½ tsp salt

¼ tsp ground turmeric

⅓ cup (79 ml) mustard oil, divided

3 green chillies

¼ cup (38 g) thinly sliced red onion

Steamed white rice (page 12), for serving

Place the fish in a bowl, sprinkle with the salt, turmeric and 1 teaspoon of the mustard oil and massage the seasonings into the fish. Allow the fish to marinate for 30 minutes.

Using a sharp knife, trim the ends of the chillies.

Place a small nonstick pan over medium heat and pour in the remaining oil. Layer a plate with a kitchen towel. Once the oil heats up, very carefully slide the fish fillets into the pan and fry for about 3 minutes on one side. Then flip and fry for 2 minutes. Using a slotted spoon, transfer the fried fillets to the kitchen towel.

Add the sliced onion and fry for about a minute. Remove from the pan with a slotted spoon. Turn off the heat and add the green chillies to the hot oil just for a few seconds. Remove using a slotted spoon.

Divide the steamed rice among three plates. Top the rice with some of the red onion and a green chilli, add some of the hot oil from the pan and place the fried fish next to it. Sprinkle with some salt and serve while it's still warm.

Chingri Aalu Boda

(Shrimp Potato Fritters)

Makes 15

Crunchy on the outside and soft inside, these fritters are ready in no time. They are typically served with rice and lentil stew but also make a great flavor-packed bite to go with drinks.

2 medium potatoes (140 g/5 oz each)

1 tbsp plus ½ tsp (20 g) salt, divided

1 tbsp plus 1 cup (252 ml) vegetable oil, divided

1 tsp grated ginger

1 tsp grated garlic

¼ cup (38 g) finely chopped onion

1 tsp ground cumin

1 tsp ground coriander

½ tsp chilli powder

7 oz (190 g) headless, peeled shrimp, finely chopped

2 tbsp (19 g) rice flour

¼ cup (30 g) breadcrumbs

Cut the potatoes in half and place in a deep saucepan. Add enough water to submerge the potatoes and then place the pan over high heat. Add 1 tablespoon (15 g) of the salt and bring the water to a boil. Then turn the heat to medium-low, and simmer the potatoes for 30 minutes. Once done, strain the boiled potatoes using a colander and allow them to cool completely. Mash the potatoes in a bowl.

Place a medium-sized, heavy-bottomed pan over medium-high heat. Heat 1 tablespoon (15 ml) of the oil, and then add the ginger, garlic and onion. Sprinkle with the remaining ½ teaspoon of salt, stir and cook for 2 minutes. Then add the cumin, coriander and chilli powder. Stir and cook for 3 more minutes. Transfer the mixture to a mixing bowl.

To the same mixing bowl, add the mashed potatoes and finely chopped shrimp. Add the rice flour and mix everything to combine. Shape about 2 tablespoons (20 g) of the mixture into a rough round dumpling. Place it on a plate and repeat with the remaining mixture.

Spread the breadcrumbs on a small plate or a bowl. Roll the dumplings in the breadcrumbs and return them to the plate.

Layer a plate with a kitchen towel and have it ready nearby.

Place a heavy-bottomed pan over medium heat and add the remaining 1 cup (237 ml) of oil. When the oil reaches 350°F (177°C), carefully add the dumplings without crowding the pan. Fry the dumplings for about 5 minutes, tossing every now and then, so they get evenly golden in color. Transfer to the kitchen towel to drain and repeat with the remaining dumplings. These taste best when served warm.

Chicken Kabiraji

(Chicken Patty Wrapped in Egg Nest)

Makes 6

This is one of Kolkata's iconic street foods and is influenced by British rule. Thinly shaped chicken patties are deep-fried and then covered in egg, creating an airy, crunchy, nest-like structure. The dish can be prepared with chicken, red meat or fish. The technique remains the same but the cooking time will change depending on what protein you are using.

Key Notes: If the patty is too thick, then wrapping around with the light egg nest will be challenging and it will break apart. So, make sure you keep the patty thin.

FOR THE CHICKEN PATTY

1 lb (500 g) ground chicken

1 egg

½ cup (76 g) finely chopped red onion

1 green chilli, finely chopped

1 tbsp (10 g) grated garlic

½ tbsp (4 g) grated ginger

1 tsp ground cumin

½ tsp garam masala

1 cup (121 g) breadcrumbs, divided

1 tsp salt

½ tsp black pepper

FOR THE EGG NEST

4 eggs

½ tsp salt

2 tbsp (30 ml) water

Oil, for deep-frying

To make the chicken patty, place the ground chicken in a mixing bowl. Crack the egg into the bowl, then add the onion, green chilli, garlic, ginger, cumin, garam masala, ¼ cup (30 g) of the breadcrumbs, salt and black pepper. Using a fork or a rubber spatula, fold together all the ingredients. Divide the mixture into 6 portions. Spread the remaining ¾ cup (91 g) of breadcrumbs on a plate. Shape each portion into about ⅔-inch (1½-cm) thick oval-shaped patties. Place each patty in the breadcrumbs and coat evenly. Set aside on a different plate to be deep-fried. Finish coating the rest of the patties.

To make the egg nest, crack the eggs into a bowl. Add the salt and water and whisk until it's smooth. Set aside.

Prepare a separate plate layered with a kitchen towel. Place a large (preferably 9-inch [23-cm]), heavy-bottomed skillet over medium heat. Pour in the oil to a depth of 1 inch (3 cm). After the oil heats up, very carefully place the prepared patties into the hot oil, without overcrowding the pan. Fry the patties for about 5 minutes or until golden brown in color. Remove from the hot oil and place on the kitchen towel to drain.

Once you are done frying all the patties, crank up the heat to medium-high. The next step is critical and needs to be done quickly. Hold the bowl with the whisked egg mixture close to the pan and, using the tip of your finger, sprinkle the mixture repeatedly over the hot oil, running your hand in one direction. You have to sprinkle several times and you have to do this step very quickly. Make sure you only sprinkle and don't pour a big lump in one shot. Sprinkling will create a thread-like texture as the egg mixture starts to fry and turn golden in color. After sprinkling several times, quickly place one of the fried patties on one edge of the fried egg strings and, using two spatulas, start rolling the chicken patty in the thread-like egg mixture. Some bits of the egg nest might break apart; just bring those together and wrap it around the chicken patty as neatly as you can. Once done, remove from the hot oil back to the kitchen towel to drain any excess oil.

Repeat the same process with rest of the chicken patties. Serve immediately.

Chicken Shingara

(Minced Chicken Wrapped in Flaky Crust)

Makes 12

I never get bored of this flaky, deep-fried, savory filled pastry. What *samosa* is to most parts of India, *shingara* is to Kolkata. The shape of a shingara is slightly smaller than that of a samosa. Filled with spiced minced chicken, dipped in ketchup and washed down with a cup of tea, this is my all-time favorite snack.

FOR THE DOUGH

1 cup (125 g) all-purpose flour

½ cup (50 g) whole wheat flour

½ tsp salt

½ tsp nigella seeds

2 tbsp (30 ml) vegetable oil

¾ cup plus 1 tbsp (195 ml) water

FOR THE FILLING

1 tbsp (15 ml) vegetable oil

1 medium red onion, finely chopped

1 tbsp (8 g) grated ginger

1 tsp grated garlic

1 tsp salt, divided

8 oz (227 g) minced chicken

½ tsp ground cumin

½ tsp ground coriander

¼ tsp chilli powder, or more to taste

1 tsp garam masala

¼ cup (38 g) frozen green peas

2 green chilli(es), chopped (optional)

Oil, for deep-frying

To make the dough, sift both the flours into a mixing bowl and add the salt and nigella seeds. Stir, add the oil and then stir to combine. Add the water little by little to form a smooth dough. Form the dough into a ball and then wrap in a damp kitchen towel. Let the dough rest for 30 minutes.

In the meantime, make the filling. Place a deep, heavy-bottomed saucepan over medium-high heat and add the oil. When the oil is hot, add the onion, ginger and garlic. Sprinkle with ½ teaspoon of the salt and stir. Cook for 2 minutes or until the onion softens. Add the minced chicken, remaining ½ teaspoon of salt, cumin, coriander and chilli powder. Cook for 10 minutes, stirring occasionally. After 10 minutes, sprinkle with the garam masala and toss in the frozen peas. Stir and cook for 5 more minutes. Check for salt and add any if you need it. Taste the mixture. If you prefer a spicier filling, add more chilli powder or 2 chopped green chillies. Once the filling is done, let it cool down before you start shaping the shingara.

To shape the shingara, knead the dough again and divide it into 6 equal portions. Then roll each portion in your palms to form smooth balls. Roll one ball into a thin, oblong shape. Using a knife, slice the rolled-out dough in half widthwise. Take one half in your hand, brush some water on the straight edges and fold the edges to form a cone, pressing the edges to seal it. Hold the cone and fill with about 2 tablespoons (29 g) of the chicken mixture. Rub some water on the edges and pinch the end to seal it tight. Allow it to sit on a cutting board to form a flat bottom. Finish shaping the rest of the shingara.

To fry the shingara, pour the oil into a deep saucepan to a depth of 3 inches (8 cm). Place the pan over medium heat. Once the oil just starts to heat up but is not hot (about 200°F [93°C]), slide the shingara carefully without crowding the pan. You will see tiny bubbles appearing on the edges of the shingara. Fry for 15 minutes, tossing and turning every few minutes until a very mild golden color. Then crank the heat to high and fry for 5 more minutes or until the shingara turns golden brown in color. Once done, using a slotted spoon, remove the shingara from the hot oil and place on a kitchen towel to drain any excess oil. Before frying the next batch of shingara, it's important to let the temperature of the oil come down to 200°F (93°C). Shingara tastes best when fresh and warm.

Dimer Devil

(Boiled Egg Wrapped with Ground Chicken)

Makes 4

Kolkata's *dimer devil* is a favorite street food. Some say that the Scotch egg inspired the dish and others say that it's a variation of the Mughal Empire's *nargisi kofta*. I think that it's a mix of both. There are a few different versions of dimer devil. Some like to scoop the yolk out, mash it with boiled potatoes, stuff it back and then deep-fry after coating the egg with breadcrumbs. I can eat eggs every day and I like the egg yolk to stay intact, which makes this my preferred version.

1 tsp olive oil

1 tbsp (8 g) grated ginger

1 tbsp (10 g) grated garlic

½ cup (76 g) finely chopped onion

1 tsp salt, divided

1 lb (454 g) ground chicken

1 tsp ground cumin

1 tsp ground coriander

1 tsp chilli powder

½ tsp garam masala

1 medium potato, peeled and boiled

¼ cup (31 g) all-purpose flour

1 egg

¼ cup (30 g) breadcrumbs

4 hard-boiled eggs, peeled

Oil, for deep-frying

Place a pan over medium-high heat and add the olive oil. When the oil is hot, add the ginger, garlic and onion. Add ½ teaspoon of the salt and stir. Cook for 2 minutes, stirring every now and then.

After 2 minutes, the onion should soften and turn a mild brown color. Add the ground chicken and stir to mix it all together. Add the remaining ½ teaspoon of salt, cumin, coriander and chilli powder. Stir and cook for 4 minutes. Make sure there are no big chunks of ground chicken. It should be broken down to a crumb-like texture. Check for salt and add any if you need it. Finally, sprinkle with the garam masala and cook for 1 minute. Turn off the heat.

Transfer the chicken mixture to a mixing bowl. Mash the boiled potato and add it to the bowl. Mix everything together to form a paste-like consistency. Divide the mixture into 4 equal patties.

Take three medium-sized shallow bowls. Spread the flour in one bowl, whisk the egg in the second bowl and spread the breadcrumbs in the third bowl.

Take one portion of the chicken-potato mixture and flatten it out. Place 1 hard-boiled egg in the center and wrap the mixture around the egg, pressing it firmly to cover the egg all around. Roll the wrapped egg in the flour, dip it into the beaten egg and then roll it in the breadcrumbs. Place it on a plate ready to deep-fry. Repeat the same process with the remaining 3 hard-boiled eggs.

Place a heavy-bottomed saucepan over medium-high heat and pour in enough oil to reach a depth of 3 inches (8 cm). Keep a plate layered with a kitchen towel ready.

When the oil reaches 300°F (150°C), very carefully add one prepared egg. Fry for about 4 minutes, turning every now and then to make sure it's evenly golden brown all over. Use a slotted spoon to remove the fried egg from the hot oil and place it on the kitchen towel. Fry the rest of the eggs. These are best served warm with a dipping sauce of your choice.

Feel-Good Food

As the name suggests, the dishes in this section are classic comfort foods that can make you feel good from the inside out. I get nostalgic every time I prepare these. Typically, Bengali meals include several courses, but when any of these dishes are prepared, I don't need anything else to follow.

Some dishes from this section can come across as spicy—there are several ways that we like to spice up the mashed potatoes and I have given my three favorite versions in this chapter. Bengalis prepare lentil soup/stew every day. Different varieties of lentils are used and prepared in numerous ways. The three humble daal recipes that I share here always take me back home.

These dishes are unpretentious and unique to Bengali cuisine. They may not come across as the prettiest plate, but they sure do taste hearty and wholesome.

Aalu Sheddho Makha

(Mashed Potatoes Three Ways)

Serves 3

We all have our comfort foods and this is almost every Bengali's all-time absolute favorite comfort food. It is our go-to meal after long days of staying out on a vacation. Warm steamed white rice (page 12) and fluffy potatoes is an unbeatable combination that is soothing to the palate and tummy. There are many different ways to uplift this utterly simple rice and potato dish and I am sharing three of my favorite versions.

3 medium potatoes

1½ tsp (8 g) salt, plus more to taste

First Version

2 tbsp (30 ml) kashundi (page 116)

1 tbsp (15 ml) mustard oil

2 dried red chillies

Second Version

3 tbsp (28 g) finely chopped red onion

3 tbsp (9 g) finely chopped fresh cilantro leaves

2 green chillies

2 tbsp (30 ml) mustard oil, divided

Third Version

2 eggs

1 tbsp (14 g) butter, melted

Clean the potatoes and cut into quarters or halves. Place a saucepan with enough cold water to cover the potatoes over high heat. Add the salt and bring the water to a boil. Then add the potatoes and lower the heat to medium. Cover the pan and cook for about 15 minutes. Then drain and peel the potatoes. Transfer to a large bowl and mash the potatoes. Divide the mashed potatoes into three equal portions to prepare three different versions of mashed potatoes.

First Version: Kashundi Aalu Makha (Mashed Potato with Raw Mango Mustard Sauce) Mix 2 tablespoons (30 ml) of *kashundi* with one portion of the mashed potatoes and taste. Add any salt if needed.

Place a small pan over medium-high heat and add 1 tablespoon (15 ml) of the mustard oil. When the oil heats up, add the dried red chillies. Allow them to sizzle for a few seconds and then pour the hot oil with the dried red chillies onto the kashundi-mashed potatoes. You could crush the red chillies and mix it in if you like. Serve warm.

Second Version: Piyaj Dhone Pata Aalu Makha (Mashed Potato with Red Onion and Cilantro Leaves) Mash the chopped onion, cilantro, green chillies and 1 tablespoon (15 ml) of the mustard oil with one portion of the mashed potatoes. Check for salt and add any if required. Pour the remaining 1 tablespoon (15 ml) of mustard oil on top and serve warm.

Third Version: Dim Aalu Makha (Mashed Potato with Boiled Eggs and Butter; this version is perfect for kids) Place the eggs into a saucepan. Add cold water to cover and bring the water to a boil. Once it's boiling, turn off the heat and cover the saucepan with a lid. Let it rest for 12 minutes for perfect hard-boiled eggs. After 2 minutes, drain the eggs and dip the boiled eggs in cold water. Remove the shells. Mash the boiled eggs with one portion of the mashed potato and the melted butter. Check for salt and add any if required. Serve warm.

Begun Poda

(Charred Eggplant Mash)

Serves 2

As the eggplant sits on the open flame, getting blistered, blackened and softened, the smoky aroma it releases is enough to make me hungry. It's then peeled and mashed with raw red onion, fresh green chillies, fresh cilantro leaves, salt and a generous glug of pungent mustard oil. No more cooking is required. Served with warm white rice (page 12), this plate is satisfactorily filling. That's the charm of charred eggplant mash.

1 medium classic globe or Italian eggplant (350 g/12 oz)

3 tbsp (45 ml) mustard oil, divided

½ cup (76 g) chopped red onion

2 green chillies, chopped

¼ cup (12 g) finely chopped fresh cilantro

1 tsp salt

Using a sharp knife, score the eggplant on all sides and rub about 1 tablespoon (15 ml) of the oil all over. Make sure some bits of oil get inside the scores. Holding the eggplant with tongs, place it over an open flame and char it all over, turning every few minutes, until the eggplant softens and the skin turns pitch black.

Place the charred eggplant in a bowl and cover the bowl with a plate or kitchen towel. The steam will make the eggplant soften further.

Once the eggplant is cooled a little bit, peel the skin off and then mash the eggplant with your hands or use a fork. Add the chopped onion, green chillies, cilantro, remaining 2 tablespoons (30 ml) of mustard oil and the salt. Give another mix with your hand or fork. Check for salt and add any if you need it.

Jhinga Baata

(Ridge Gourd Spicy Mash)

Serves 2

Baata means "mash," and Bengalis use different vegetables to make this satisfying dish. It may not come across as one of the prettiest looking foods, but it sure does provide a feeling of utter comfort. This is one dish that I would always ask Ma to prepare on days when I felt ill and a hearty meal was all that my palate craved.

1 large ridge gourd

1 tbsp (15 ml) mustard oil, divided

2 dried red chillies

1 tsp grated ginger

1 tbsp (10 g) grated garlic

1 or 2 green chillies, finely chopped

1 small red onion, finely chopped

¼ tsp salt, plus more if needed

½ tsp ground turmeric

Steamed white rice (page 12), for serving

Peel the pointy ends of the ridge gourd and then cut it into big chunks. Place in a saucepan, add water to cover and place the pan over high heat. Once the water starts to boil, turn the heat to medium and allow it to simmer for 10 minutes or until the ridge gourd is tender.

Using a colander, drain the boiled ridge gourd and then finely chop it using a knife or put it in a food processor and pulse it a few times. You want it a little chunky and not like a paste. Set aside.

Place another pan over medium heat and add ½ tablespoon (7 ml) of the oil. Add the dried red chillies and allow them to sizzle for a few seconds.

Add the ginger, garlic, 1 green chilli (or 2 if you like it spicier) and onion. Sprinkle with the salt and the turmeric. Stir and cook for 5 minutes, stirring occasionally and making sure it doesn't burn on the bottom.

After 5 minutes, when the raw smell is gone, add the finely chopped boiled ridge gourd. Stir and continue cooking for 5 more minutes. Check for salt and add any if required.

Drizzle with the remaining ½ tablespoon (7 ml) of mustard oil, stir and serve warm with rice.

Cholar Daal

(Split Bengal Gram Stew)

Serves 4

Split Bengal gram (*cholar daal*) is very commonly confused with split pigeon peas (*toor daal*). They both look very similar, except that the Bengal gram is chunkier and doesn't cook down to a creamy or mushy consistency. It retains its shape and tastes sweeter than any other kind of lentils. Flavored with *paanch phoron* and sweetened with a hint of sugar and coconut flakes, cholar daal is hearty and often prepared on special occasions. Served with *luchi* (deep-fried puffed mini bread, page 17) and *beguni* (crispy eggplant slices, page 37), it makes a favorite weekend breakfast.

1 cup (200 g) split Bengal gram

3 cups (710 ml) water

½ tsp salt, plus more to taste

1 tbsp (15 ml) oil

3 green cardamom pods

1 tbsp (6 g) paanch phoron (page 11)

2 bay leaves

½ tsp ground turmeric

3 green chillies, finely chopped

1 tsp sugar

½ inch (1 cm) ginger, peeled and grated

¼ cup (19 g) toasted coconut flakes

Fill a large bowl with cold water and add the lentils. Using your hands, scrub the lentils to clean off any dust. Using a colander, drain the lentils and wash them in several changes of water. Soak the washed lentils in water overnight.

Next, pour the water into a large, heavy-bottomed saucepan and add the washed lentils and the salt. Stir and place the saucepan over high heat.

In 2 minutes, the water will come to a boil. Turn down the heat to medium, and allow the lentils to simmer for 30 minutes or until the lentils are cooked through but still retain their shape.

Place another heavy-bottomed pan over medium heat and add the oil. Once the oil heats up, add the cardamom pods, *paanch phoron* and bay leaves. Give it a couple of seconds for the spices to sizzle and infuse the oil. Now add the lentils, turmeric and green chillies. Stir and let it cook for a couple of minutes. Add more water if the consistency looks too thick.

Sprinkle with the sugar, ginger and half of the toasted coconut flakes. Check for salt and add any, if required.

Sprinkle the remaining toasted coconut flakes on top and serve warm.

Narkol Aar Till Baata

(Coconut and Sesame Mash)

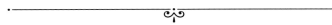

Serves 2

The combination of freshly grated sweet coconut and nutty white sesame seeds makes a tasty creamy mash. To balance that sweetness, in goes some tangy tamarind, pungent mustard oil and dried red chillies. This is yet another mash that I go for on days when my palate wants something out of the ordinary. It is typically enjoyed with steamed white rice (page 12), but you could serve it as a dip instead with crackers or fritters or as a spread on tortillas.

⅓ cup (54 g) white sesame seeds

¼ cup (19 g) fresh or frozen grated coconut

1 tbsp (16 g) tamarind paste

1 tsp sugar

½ tsp salt

1 tbsp (15 ml) mustard oil

2 dried red chillies

½ tsp black mustard seeds

Use a small blender or a mortar and pestle to grind the sesame seeds, grated coconut, tamarind paste, sugar and salt. Add 1 tablespoon (15 ml) of water if you find it too dry to blend. Transfer to a bowl and set aside.

Place a small pan over high heat and add the oil. Once the oil is hot, turn off the heat and carefully add the dried red chillies and mustard seeds. Let them sizzle for a few seconds and then pour it on top of the blended coconut and sesame mixture. Stir. Taste for salt and add any if required.

Ilish Maach Er Matha Diye Daal

(Hilsa Fish Head Lentil Stew)

Serves 2

Most parts of India don't consume fish head. Bengalis, on the other hand, consider it a delicacy and always relish it in several different ways. It's cooked in lentil stew, with rice and sometimes stir-fried with vegetables. My favorite way to enjoy hilsa fish head is always in a light lentil stew. The stew is mildly spiced and the major portion of the aroma comes from the hilsa fish head.

Key Notes: You don't have to restrict this dish to just hilsa fish head. You can try it with any other variety of fish head too.

1 hilsa fish head, cut in half

1 tsp salt, divided

1 tsp turmeric, divided

½ cup (100 g) skinned and split mung beans

2 cups (473 ml) water

½ cup plus 1 tbsp (133 ml) oil, divided

3 bay leaves

½ tsp cumin seeds

3 fresh green or red chillies, sliced in half

1 tbsp (8 g) grated ginger

2 lime wedges

Steamed white rice (page 12), for serving

Place the fish head in a bowl and sprinkle with ½ teaspoon of the salt and ½ teaspoon of the turmeric. Using your hands, massage the fish head to coat it all over with the salt and turmeric. Allow it to marinate while you boil the mung beans.

Place a pan over medium-high heat and when it heats up, add the mung beans. Dry roast the beans for 5 minutes, turning them every now and then, so they get evenly roasted. Once you see the shade of the beans changes to mild brown, transfer to a heavy-bottomed saucepan.

Add the water to the saucepan and place it over high heat. Sprinkle with the remaining ½ teaspoon of salt. Once the water comes to a boil, turn down the heat to medium and allow it to simmer for 40 minutes or until the beans are softened. Remove from the heat and set aside.

Now place a medium-sized wok or deep skillet over medium-high heat and add the ½ cup (118 ml) of oil. When the oil heats up, carefully add the fish head and fry for 3 minutes on each side. Transfer to a plate layered with a kitchen towel.

To make the stew you could either use the same pan or use a separate one. If you are using the same pan, then remove most of the leftover fried oil from the pan and leave 1 tablespoon (15 ml). Or take a fresh pan, place it over medium heat and add the remaining 1 tablespoon (15 ml) of oil.

When the oil heats up, add the bay leaves, cumin seeds and chillies. After a few seconds, add the remaining ½ teaspoon of turmeric and the grated ginger. Cook for 1 minute and then pour the boiled mung beans into the pan. Stir and cook for 3 minutes. If it gets too thick, add water to thin it out.

Next, carefully add the fried fish head and cook for 5 minutes. Squeeze fresh lime juice on top and serve the stew warm with steamed white rice.

Piyaj Mushuri Daal

(Caramelized Onion Red Lentil Soup)

Serves 2

Mushuri daal is one of the most common lentil stews prepared on a daily basis, mainly because this variety of lentils cooks really fast. The sweetness of the caramelized onion with the pungent bitter taste of nigella seeds makes this *piyaj mushuri daal* unlike any other. This is one of those *daals* that I like to keep light and runny.

Key Notes: The star of this lentil soup is the caramelized onion. It's important to fry the sliced onion until golden brown without rushing through this step.

1 large red onion

¼ cup (50 g) split red lentils

3¼ cups (769 ml) water, divided

1 tsp salt, divided

2 tbsp (30 ml) vegetable oil

1 tsp nigella seeds

2 dried red chillies

½ tsp ground turmeric

Steamed white rice (page 12), for serving

Lemon wedges

Using a sharp knife, carefully slice off the bottom and top part of the onion. Now place the onion on one edge and cut it in half. Peel off the skin and discard. Place half the onion, cut side down, on a chopping board and, holding firmly, slice vertically into thin slices. Set it aside to be used later.

Fill a large bowl with cold water and add the lentils. Using your hands, scrub the lentils to clean off any dust. The water will turn milky. Using a colander, drain the lentils and wash them in several changes of water.

Next, add 3 cups (710 ml) of the water to a large, heavy-bottomed saucepan and add the washed lentils and ½ teaspoon of the salt. Stir and place the saucepan over high heat.

In 2 minutes, the water will come to a boil. Turn down the heat to medium and allow the lentils to simmer for 15 to 17 minutes or until the lentils are cooked through and mash easily when pressed with a spoon. Remove from the heat and set aside.

Simultaneously, heat a 9-inch (23-cm) nonstick wok or deep pan over medium-high heat and add the vegetable oil. Add the nigella seeds and dried red chillies and let them sizzle for 2 seconds. Next, add the thinly sliced red onion. Sprinkle with the remaining ½ teaspoon of salt and the turmeric and stir. Lower the heat to medium and continue cooking the onion, stirring occasionally, for 15 minutes or until it's caramelized to a golden brown color.

Add the cooked lentils and remaining ¼ cup (59 ml) of water, stir and cook for 2 minutes to heat through. Taste and add any salt if required.

Serve with steamed rice and a squeeze of fresh lemon juice.

Panta Bhaat

(Fermented Leftover Steamed White Rice)

Serves 4

This is one of those long-lost recipes that people don't bother to prepare much. Often, the leftover rice gets tossed in a hot wok to prepare fried rice. But the most common old-fashioned way is to soak the leftover rice in water and let it ferment for several hours. Then, enjoy it with several sides like *Mushuri Daal Er Boda* (Red Lentil Fritters, page 38), *Begun Poda* (Charred Eggplant Mash, page 60) or/and *Ilish Maach Bhaja* (Deep-Fried Hilsa Fish, page 46). Irrespective of what side you choose, don't forget to dry roast some red chillies in a hot pan or over an open flame. The soothing fermented white rice gets uplifted with the smoky flavor of the dried red chillies.

2 cups (322 g) leftover steamed white rice (page 12)

2 cups (473 ml) water

½ tsp salt

3 dried red chillies

¼ cup (38 g) thinly sliced red onion

Place the rice and water in a large bowl. Using your hands, massage the rice to make sure the grains are separated so they will soak completely. Add more water if needed. Cover the bowl and let the rice ferment for 12 hours.

After 12 hours, using your hands, crush the rice grains a little bit. If you prefer it smoother, then crush the rice grains further. Sprinkle with the salt and stir.

Place a dry pan over medium-high heat and roast the dried red chillies until they turn a shade darker.

Crush the dry-roasted red chillies over the fermented rice, add the sliced red onion and serve with your favorite sides.

Plant-Based Main Dishes

The definition of "vegetarian" in Bengali is different from the rest of India. Most Indians who eat vegetarian do not consume fish, meat or eggs. But the Bengali term "vegetarian" goes a little beyond that. In addition to fish, meat and eggs, onion and garlic are also omitted.

People tend to think that it's impossible for Bengalis to enjoy plant-based food because we lean toward nonvegetarian meals. The fact is, there are Bengalis who live on vegetarian meals and there are Bengalis who love their vegetarian dishes as much as they savor meat and fish.

In a typical daily five-course meal, there are at least two courses of vegetarian dishes. These plant-based dishes have a wide variety of terms that start with the name of the vegetable followed by the term *torkari, dalna, chechki, ghanta* or *labra*. It may sound confusing—and it is even to most Bengalis—but if you break it down, these dishes are either stir-fried or cooked in a light gravy or in a thick stew. The key point to remember is that all these pure vegetarian dishes are subtly flavored with a few whole spices and a couple of green chillies.

Typically, most Bengali families dedicate one day of the week to eating pure vegetarian. Ma was quite strict with this rule, and growing up, I remember our kitchen being divided into two sections with two sets of utensils and two different stoves, vegetarian and nonvegetarian. Of course, with age, she has found it difficult to maintain it to that extent. But on those pure vegetarian days, she still doesn't allow us to prepare anything nonvegetarian. She prepares several courses of mildly spiced dishes using *chaana* (fresh cheese, page 13), seasonal vegetables and fruits.

This chapter includes some of the most common plant-based meals that are prepared on a day-to-day basis. All these dishes are typically served with *bhaat* (steamed white rice, page 12) or *ruti* (whole wheat Indian flatbread, page 14).

Shukto

(Mixed Vegetable Bittersweet Stew)

Serves 4

Shukto is a medley of vegetables that are slow cooked until they are tender but still hold their shape. It's a mildly spiced stew with a hint of bitterness from the bitter gourd. It's always served right at the beginning of a meal. The bitterness works as a palate cleanser, which makes a good start for the meal to follow. A generous amount of freshly grated ginger goes right at the end of cooking for that punch in the palate. There are quite a few versions of this dish and you could pick any seasonal vegetables that you prefer. This dish tastes best with steamed white rice (page 12).

1 small ridge gourd (150 g/5 oz)

1 plantain (113 g/4 oz)

Italian or classic globe eggplant (150 g/5 oz)

1 bitter gourd (113 g/4 oz)

12 to 15 green beans

1 tbsp (15 ml) oil

2 dried red chillies

½ tsp black mustard seeds

Salt to taste

½ tsp sugar

¼ tsp ground turmeric

1 cup (237 ml) water

1 tsp grated ginger

¼ cup (59 ml) milk

Peel the pointy ends of the ridge gourd and peel the plantain. Trim the ends of the eggplant and the bitter gourd. Dice all the vegetables into big chunks (about ¾ inch [2 cm]). Cut the green beans into 1-inch (3-cm) lengths.

Place a heavy-bottomed pan over medium heat and add the oil. When the oil starts to heat up, add the dried red chillies and mustard seeds. Once they begin to sizzle, add the chunks of vegetables and stir.

Sprinkle with the salt, sugar and turmeric. Stir. Cook for 2 minutes over medium heat and then add the water. Cover the pan and continue cooking over medium-low heat until the vegetables have softened, about 10 minutes.

Once the vegetables are tender, add the grated ginger. At this point taste for salt and add any if required. Add the milk and cook for 1 more minute. Turn off the heat and cover the pan. Let it rest for a couple minutes before you serve it warm.

Bandhakopir Torkari

(Cabbage Potato Stir-Fry with Mustard and Poppy Seeds)

Serves 2

Unlike most cabbage stir-fry dishes, this particular recipe calls for chunky pieces of cabbage. It is cooked in minimal spices until softened and finished with a mustard and poppy seed paste. This paste adds a subtle creamy, pungent flavor to the whole dish, which is unlike any cabbage stir-fried dish you might have tried.

1 medium potato

½ head cabbage

2 tsp (6 g) mustard seeds

1 tsp white poppy seeds

1 green chilli

¾ cup plus 1 tbsp (192 ml) water, divided

1 tsp vegetable oil

1 tsp nigella seeds

2 dried red chillies

½ tsp salt, divided

½ tsp ground turmeric, divided

Peel the potato and slice it in half lengthwise. Then slice the halves into wedges and each wedge into bite-size chunks.

Place the cabbage half cut-side down, slice it into 3 equal portions lengthwise and then slice each portion into bite-size chunks.

Using a spice or coffee grinder, coarsely grind the mustard seeds and poppy seeds separately. Add the coarsely ground seeds to a mortar and pestle along with the green chilli and 1 tablespoon (15 ml) of the water. Pound it to form a smooth paste. Set aside.

Place a pan over medium-high heat and add the oil. When the oil heats up, add the nigella seeds and dried red chillies. After a couple of seconds of sizzling, add the sliced potatoes, ¼ teaspoon of the salt and ¼ teaspoon of the turmeric. Stir and cook for 3 minutes, stirring now and then.

After 3 minutes, add the sliced cabbage, remaining ¼ teaspoon of salt and remaining ¼ teaspoon of turmeric. Stir and cook for 1 minute.

Add ½ cup (118 ml) of the water, stir, cover the pan, lower the heat to medium-low and cook for 5 minutes or until the potatoes are cooked through and tender. The cabbage slices should be tender but not mushy.

Finally, add the remaining ¼ cup (59 ml) of water to the mustard and poppy seed paste and pour it into the pan. Stir and cook for 3 more minutes. Check for salt at this stage and add any if required. Serve warm.

Dudh Phulkopi

(Cauliflower in Mild Spiced Milk Gravy)

Serves 4

I grew up eating a lot of cauliflower. It was prepared at least twice a week. There are various ways we cook this vegetable. This particular dish I learned from Ma while I was writing this book. It's a dish that my grandma used to prepare on busy days, when she needed a curry in a hurry. Like most pure vegetarian dishes, this too is subtly spiced. Cooking the cauliflower in milk makes it light and very soothing to the palate.

1 head cauliflower

3 tbsp plus 1 tsp (35 ml) oil, divided

1½ tsp (8 g) salt

½ tsp ground turmeric

1 tsp nigella seeds

1 bay leaf

3 green cardamom pods

1 cup (237 ml) milk

2 green chillies

Using a sharp knife, cut the cauliflower into bite-size florets and wash under running water. Place a heavy-bottomed pan over medium-high heat with enough water to cover the florets. When the water comes to a boil, add the florets and boil for 5 minutes. Drain the florets using a colander and set aside.

Place a heavy-bottomed skillet over medium heat. Add 3 tablespoons (15 ml) of the oil. When the oil heats up, add the cauliflower florets, salt and turmeric. Fry the florets for 5 to 7 minutes. Remove from the hot pan.

To the same pan, heat 1 teaspoon of the oil and add the nigella seeds, bay leaf and cardamom. Stir, and then add the milk and fried cauliflower florets. Add the green chillies and cook for 5 minutes, stirring occasionally. Check for salt and add any if required. Serve warm.

Shoshar Torkari

(Cucumber Ginger Stir-Fry)

Serves 2

This is one of my absolute favorite pure vegetarian dishes. Sweet cucumber is cooked until tender and then uplifted with a good dose of fresh ginger. A generous sprinkling of fresh cilantro leaves and it's ready to serve. Every time I visit home, this is one of the dishes I always ask Ma to make. It's also a quick go-to meal for busy weeknights.

1 large cucumber

1 tbsp (15 ml) oil

1 tsp black mustard seeds

1 dry red chilli

1 tsp salt

1 tsp sugar

½ tsp ground turmeric

1 tbsp (8 g) grated ginger

⅓ cup (17 g) finely chopped fresh cilantro

Peel the cucumber and finely dice it.

Place a heavy-bottomed pan over medium heat and add the oil. Add the mustard seeds and dry red chilli and allow them to sizzle for 2 seconds. Add the diced cucumber very carefully and stir. Sprinkle on the salt, sugar and turmeric. Stir. Turn the heat to medium-low, cover the pan and allow it to simmer for 10 minutes.

Once the cucumber is cooked through, add the freshly grated ginger and the finely chopped fresh cilantro. Give a toss and cook for 2 more minutes. Serve warm.

Zucchini Aalu Posto

(Zucchini and Potato Stir-Fried with Poppy Seeds)

Serves 2

Using poppy seeds in curry is very common in Bengali cooking. It adds a nutty aroma and a subtle creaminess to the dish. One of the most common poppy seed dishes is *aalu posto* (potatoes with poppy seeds), which is made with just potatoes. Sometimes green veggies like green beans or ridge gourd are added as well to make a different variety. I like the combination of zucchini with potatoes. The key is not to cook down the veggies too much.

10 baby potatoes, cut in half

1½ tsp (8 g) salt, divided

1 medium green zucchini

3 tbsp (25 g) white poppy seeds

¼ cup (19 g) fresh or frozen grated coconut

1 green chilli

1 tbsp plus ½ cup (133 ml) water, divided

1 tsp vegetable oil

1 tbsp (8 g) nigella seeds

2 dried red chillies

½ tsp ground turmeric

½ tsp sugar

Pour enough water into a pot to boil the potatoes and bring the water to a boil over high heat. Then add the potatoes and 1 teaspoon of the salt and turn down the heat to medium. Cover the pan and boil for 5 to 8 minutes or until the potatoes are fork-tender but not mushy. Once done, drain the potatoes using a colander and then let them cool completely before you peel them.

Slice the zucchini in half lengthwise. Cut the halves into bite-size half-moon slices, about ¾ inch (2 cm) thick.

Place a pan over medium-high heat and when hot, dry roast the poppy seeds for a few seconds. Using a mortar and pestle or a small blender, blend the roasted poppy seeds, grated coconut, green chilli and 1 tablespoon (15 ml) of the water into a smooth paste. Set aside.

Place a heavy-bottomed pan over medium heat and add the oil. When the oil is hot, add the nigella seeds and dried red chillies. Let them sizzle for a few seconds and then add the potatoes and zucchini. Sprinkle on the remaining ½ teaspoon of salt, turmeric and sugar. Stir and cook for 5 minutes.

Add the poppy seed and coconut paste and the remaining ½ cup (118 ml) of water. Cook for 5 more minutes and check for salt. Add any if required. Serve warm.

Doi Begun

(Eggplant Chunks in Spiced Yogurt)

Serves 4

Eggplant is one of those veggies that I never get bored of. This is a dish that I prepare quite often with barely any leftovers. Typically, this dish is prepared by cooking the yogurt and spices together before adding the pan-fried eggplant. I like to prepare it a little differently. I spoon the spiced yogurt mixture onto the fried eggplant and then add the hot-tempered oil on top.

Key Notes: The dish tastes best when prepared and served immediately. If you warm the dish in the microwave, the yogurt will loosen its texture and the taste will not be the same.

1 medium Italian or classic globe eggplant (200 g/7 oz)

2 tsp (10 g) salt, divided

1 tsp ground turmeric

2 tbsp and 2 tsp (35 ml) oil, divided

1 tsp cumin seeds

2 cups (490 g) thick Greek yogurt

1 tsp sugar

10 fresh curry leaves

1 tsp black mustard seeds

1 tsp chilli powder

Cut the eggplant into slices about ⅓ inch (1 cm) thick. Depending on the shape of the eggplant, you could either slice it into circles or half-moons. Then rub 1 teaspoon of the salt and the turmeric on both sides of the eggplant slices. Layer them on a plate and let rest for 30 minutes.

After 30 minutes, the eggplant will have softened and released some moisture. Take a kitchen towel and dab it on both sides of the eggplant to remove the excess moisture.

Place a nonstick pan over medium heat and add 2 tablespoons (30 ml) of the oil. Spread the oil evenly and, when the oil gets hot, layer on the eggplant slices. Using a spatula, press the slices lightly and cook for about 2 minutes on each side. Once you are done frying the eggplant, remove from the hot pan and layer on a serving plate.

Place a separate small pan over high heat and dry roast the cumin seeds for a few seconds. Then grind it to a fine powder using a coffee grinder or a mortar and pestle.

In a small mixing bowl, combine the yogurt, ground cumin, remaining 1 teaspoon of salt and the sugar. Whisk to blend.

Place the small pan back over medium-high heat and add the remaining 2 teaspoons (10 ml) of oil. When the oil heats up, turn off the heat and, very carefully, leaning back away from the pan, add the curry leaves, black mustard seeds and chilli powder. It will splatter and sizzle. Swirl the pan and then pour half of the the hot infused oil into the yogurt mixture. Stir to combine.

Pour the yogurt mixture on top of the fried eggplant, coating all the slices. Toss gently to mix all the eggplant slices with the spiced yogurt sauce. Pour the remaining infused oil on top. Allow it to sit for 15 minutes and then serve.

Chaana Kaju Torkari

(Cottage Cheese Dumplings in Creamy Cashew Gravy)

Serves 2

If you are familiar with Indian cooking, you must be aware of *paneer*, or Indian cottage cheese. *Chaana* is the fresh cottage cheese that is pressed to make paneer. In Bengali cooking, fresh chaana is used a lot in savory dishes. Instead of pressing the fresh cheese to form chunks of paneer, it's kneaded and then rolled into dumplings. The most common way to prepare a chaana stew is with potato chunks in a mildly-spiced gravy. I like to prepare it a little differently with creamy cashew and yogurt.

1 cup (230 g) chaana (page 13)

1 tbsp (8 g) all-purpose flour

½ tsp ground turmeric, divided

1 tsp salt, divided

10 cashews

¼ cup (61 g) thick Greek yogurt

3 tbsp (45 ml) oil, divided

1-inch (3-cm) cinnamon stick

3 green cardamom pods

2 bay leaves

1 tbsp (8 g) grated ginger

½ cup (123 g) tomato puree

½ tsp sugar

¼ tsp chilli powder

1 tbsp (8 g) bhaja moshla (page 11)

½ cup (118 ml) water

½ tsp gorom moshla (page 11)

2 tbsp (6 g) finely chopped fresh cilantro leaves

Place the fresh chaana on a plate or chopping board and knead it like you would knead bread dough. Knead it for about 7 minutes or until the fresh chaana feels soft and your palms feel a little oily. Once done, sprinkle with the flour, ¼ teaspoon of the turmeric and ½ teaspoon of the salt. Knead again to mix everything together. Divide the dough into 10 portions and make smooth round dumplings out of the dough. Flatten the dumplings lightly and set aside on a plate.

Using a spice blender, grind the cashews to a fine powder. Combine the yogurt and cashew powder in a bowl and set aside.

Place a nonstick pan over medium heat and add 2 tablespoons (30 ml) of the oil. When the oil heats up, carefully layer the chaana dumplings and fry for 1 minute on each side. Remove from the pan and set aside on a plate.

In the same pan, heat the remaining 1 tablespoon (15 ml) of oil and add the cinnamon stick, cardamom and bay leaves. Allow them to sizzle for a few seconds and then add the grated ginger and tomato puree. Sprinkle on the sugar, remaining ½ teaspoon of salt, remaining ¼ teaspoon of turmeric, chilli powder and *bhaja moshla*. Stir and cook for 5 minutes.

Add the yogurt and cashew mixture and cook for 3 minutes, stirring constantly. Add the water, fried chaana and gorom moshla and simmer for 5 minutes.

Sprinkle with the fresh cilantro leaves and serve warm.

Fish, Meat and Egg Main Dishes

Many rivers and seas surround West Bengal, making seafood the leading protein in a typical Bengali diet. A common term that is used to describe us is *"Mache Bhaate Bangali,"* literally translating to "Fish Rice Bengalis." Twice a week, Baba would visit the fish market early in the morning with the plan to get some fresh fish for lunch. No frozen fish was allowed at home. Unlike many other cuisines, we eat every part of the fish.

Fish also holds a great significance in most of our ceremonies. During weddings, the bride's family will send a huge fish all styled up with colorful paper and glitter to the groom's family as part of the gift ritual. During the *Annaprashan* at six months, babies taste not only *payesh* (see page 131) as their first solid food but also get a taste of fish. The practice starts that early! Fish is considered almost as auspicious as rice. Fish is prepared in numerous ways based on the type of fish, its oil content, size and the amount of bones present. Preparing fish is nearly an everyday affair, except on the days when we eat pure vegetarian meals.

Although fish holds first place, poultry, meat and eggs aren't too far behind. Chicken and mutton are most often reserved for weekends and gatherings. Baba would put on his chef's hat that day, giving Ma a much-needed break. Egg curries are often a favorite of children, so whenever Ma would prepare a spicy fish curry, there was also egg curry for us kids. I follow the same ritual as well. My little fella loves eggs, so an egg curry means dinnertime is quick and fuss free.

The dishes in this chapter are typically served as a main course, often with *bhaat* (steamed white rice, page 12) or *ruti* (whole wheat Indian flatbread, page 14).

Tomato Kalojeera Maach Er Jhol

(Tomato and Nigella Seed Fish Stew)

Serves 4

This is an everyday fish stew that is prepared more often than any other. Very mildly spiced with nigella seeds and few green chillies, this is a simple stew and takes barely any time to prepare. The flavor combination of nigella seeds with tangy tomato works beautifully. Most often, this dish is prepared with *rohu* fish, but you can try catfish or salmon too.

Key Notes: Depending on the kind of fish you are using, the frying time will differ. Typically, fish are deep-fried before adding to a stew, but if you are using salmon or catfish, shallow panfrying for a couple of minutes should be enough.

4 rohu fish steaks

1½ tsp (8 g) salt, divided

1 tsp ground turmeric, divided

1 medium red onion

1 tomato

Oil, for deep-frying

1 tsp nigella seeds

½ tsp sugar

3 green chillies

1½ cups (355 ml) water

¼ cup (12 g) finely chopped fresh cilantro leaves

Place the fish steaks in a bowl and sprinkle with 1 teaspoon of the salt and ½ teaspoon of the turmeric. Massage the seasonings into the fish steaks.

Peel the onion and thinly slice it. Thinly slice the tomato. Set aside.

Place a heavy-bottomed pan over medium heat and pour in the oil to reach a depth of 1 inch (3 cm). Layer a plate with kitchen towels. Once the oil heats up, carefully add the fish steaks and cover the pan because it might splatter. Allow the steaks to fry for 3 minutes, then flip over and fry for 2 more minutes. Transfer the fish to the kitchen towel with a slotted spoon.

To prepare the curry you could use the same pan by removing most of the oil except for 1 teaspoon. Or place a separate pan over medium heat and pour in 1 teaspoon of oil.

When the oil heats up, sprinkle in the nigella seeds and stir. Add the sliced onion, the remaining ½ teaspoon of salt, the remaining ½ teaspoon of turmeric and the sugar. Stir and cook for about 5 minutes.

Add the tomato slices and stir. Trim the ends off the green chillies and add them, too. Cook for 5 minutes, then add the water. Stir and bring the water to a boil. Cook for 2 minutes, then carefully layer the fried fish steaks in the sauce and continue cooking for 3 more minutes.

Check for salt and add any if required. Add the chopped cilantro leaves, stir and it's ready to serve.

Rui Maach Er Kalia

(Rohu Fish in Sweet and Spicy Tomato Sauce)

Serves 4

This is one of those dishes that makes a mandatory appearance on special occasions. It is rich in flavor because of the perfect balance of sweet and spicy. Unlike most fish stews, the gravy is thick and I like to add some powdered cashews at the end for extra sweetness and creaminess.

4 rohu fish steaks

1½ tsp (8 g) salt, divided

1 tsp ground turmeric, divided

1 red onion

1 tbsp (8 g) grated ginger

1 tbsp (10 g) grated garlic

4 green chillies

1 cup plus 1 tbsp (252 ml) oil, divided

3 green cardamom pods

1-inch (3-cm) cinnamon stick

5 cloves

½ cup (123 g) tomato puree, or 2 tbsp (31 g) tomato paste plus 2 tbsp (30 ml) water

1 tsp sugar

1 tsp ground cumin

1 tsp ground coriander

½ tsp chilli powder

½ tsp gorom moshla (page 11)

2 tbsp (15 g) powdered cashews

½ cup (118 ml) water

Place the fish steaks on a plate. Sprinkle with ½ teaspoon of the salt and ½ teaspoon of the turmeric. Using your hands, massage the seasonings into the fish to coat on all sides. Let rest for 30 minutes.

Peel the onion and slice it in half. Cut one half into thin half-moon slices. Very finely chop the other half, place in a bowl, add the ginger and garlic and stir to combine. Set both portions of onion aside.

Trim the ends of the green chillies and set aside. Place a nonstick heavy-bottomed 8-inch (20-cm) pan over medium-high heat and add 1 cup (237 ml) of the oil. Prepare a plate with layers of kitchen towels. When the oil gets hot, carefully place the marinated fish steaks in the pan. Do not overcrowd the pan. Cook for 2 minutes on each side. Transfer the fish steaks to the plate with the kitchen towels to drain.

To prepare the curry, you need 1 tablespoon (15 ml) of oil. So, you could either remove the excess oil from the same pan and retain just 1 tablespoon (15 ml) or use a separate pan and add the remaining 1 tablespoon (15 ml) of oil to it. Place the pan over medium heat. When the oil gets hot, crush the green cardamom and add to the pan along with the cinnamon stick and cloves. Allow them to sizzle for a few seconds, and then add the thinly sliced onion. Sprinkle ½ teaspoon of salt and the remaining ½ teaspoon of turmeric. Stir and cook for 3 minutes. Add the onion, garlic and ginger mixture, stir and cook for 5 minutes.

Add the tomato puree or the tomato paste. If you are using tomato paste, add 2 tablespoons (30 ml) of water to the pan and stir. Add the sugar, remaining ½ teaspoon of salt, cumin, coriander and chilli powder. Cook for 3 minutes, stirring every now and then. Add the gorom moshla and powdered cashews and stir. Cook for 2 minutes. Next, add the water, stir and nestle the fried fish steaks and green chillis in the sauce. Crank up the heat to medium-high. It will start to splatter, so cover the pan and cook for 3 minutes. Then carefully remove the pan from the heat, flip the fish steaks and cook for 2 more minutes. Check for salt and add any if required. Serve warm.

Aalu Begun Diye Papda Maach Er Jhol

(Potato and Eggplant Pabo Catfish Stew)

Serves 4

Starchy potatoes and creamy eggplant make a great combination for a light stew perfect for warm days. It's very mildly spiced with just a sprinkle of pungent nigella seeds and the light spice blend of *bhaja moshla* at the end. The stew can be prepared with a variety of fish, but with the delicate pabo catfish, the stew comes out hearty without much effort at all.

Key Notes: If you can't find pabo catfish, use another mild-flavored fish.

4 papda maach (pabo catfish), cleaned

1 tsp salt, divided

1 tsp ground turmeric, divided

¼ cup plus 1 tsp (64 ml) oil, divided

1 small potato

1 classic globe or Italian eggplant (200 g/7 oz)

1 tsp nigella seeds

1 tsp bhaja moshla (page 11)

1¾ cups plus 1 tbsp (429 ml) water, divided

3 green chillies, sliced in half

1 tsp all-purpose flour

Fresh cilantro for garnish

Place the fish on a plate and sprinkle with ½ teaspoon of the salt, ½ teaspoon of the turmeric and 1 teaspoon of the oil. Massage the seasonings into the fish with your hands and set aside for 30 minutes.

Peel the potato and slice it into wedges. Slice the eggplant to a similar size and shape as the potato. Keep the sliced potato and sliced eggplant in separate bowls. Then sprinkle the remaining ½ teaspoon of salt and remaining ½ teaspoon of turmeric on both bowls and massage the seasonings into the potatoes and eggplant.

Place a heavy-bottomed 9-inch (23-cm) pan over medium heat and add the remaining ¼ cup (59 ml) of vegetable oil. When the oil is hot, very carefully add the fish to the pan because the oil will splatter. Do not overcrowd the pan; you may need to fry the fish in batches. Fry the fish for 2 minutes on each side, then transfer to a separate plate with a slotted spoon. If there is excess oil in the pan, pour it into a bowl, retaining 1 teaspoon.

Sprinkle the nigella seeds in the hot oil and once they start to sizzle, mix the bhaja moshla with 1 tablespoon (15 ml) of the water and pour it into the pan. Stir and cook for 2 minutes, then add the potatoes. Stir and cook the potatoes for 5 minutes, then add the eggplant slices. Stir and cook for 3 minutes, then add 1½ cups (355 ml) of water. Crank up the heat and bring the water to a boil. Once it comes to a boil, turn down the heat to medium, add the green chillies, cover the pan and continue simmering for 3 minutes or until the potatoes are cooked through. Then add the fried fish and very gently toss around so the gravy covers the fish.

In a small bowl, mix the remaining ¼ cup (59 ml) of water and the flour to a smooth consistency, then pour it into the pan. This will thicken the gravy. Cook for 2 minutes and add salt if required. Garnish with chopped fresh cilantro and serve warm.

Kashundi Ilish Paturi

(Hilsa Fish with Mustard Sauce Wrapped in Banana Leaf)

Serves 4

Paturi comes from the Bengali word *paata*, meaning "leaves." Fish coated with a spice paste and wrapped in a banana leaf is a style of cooking that many countries follow. There are various ways to prepare this dish. Some prefer to steam it and others prefer to pan roast it or grill it over an open flame. The mustard sauce (*shorshe baata*) filling is always a favorite, but I like it more with a homemade tangy *kashundi*. Once the hot parcels are opened, the pungent aroma comes through immediately, almost clearing your sinuses. This entire meal is quite easy to put together if you have some kashundi in stock.

Key Notes: Hilsa fish can be replaced by salmon, catfish, bass or tilapia. Although the aroma will not be the same, you will still get the essence of the dish.

1 cup (245 g) kashundi (page 116)

½ cup (123 g) thick Greek yogurt

4 hilsa fillets

4 banana leaves, each 10" x 20" (20 x 40 cm)

2 tbsp (30 ml) mustard oil, divided

4 green chillies

Steamed white rice (page 12) for serving

In a bowl, whisk together the kashundi and yogurt.

Clean the fish fillets and place on a plate. Pour some of the kashundi yogurt mixture on the fish fillets and use your hands to coat the fish evenly on both sides, including the cavity. Set aside for 15 minutes.

Wipe the banana leaves clean with a damp kitchen towel. Then take 1 tablespoon (15 ml) of the mustard oil in your hand and rub it on the leaves. Next, place a skillet over medium-low heat and when the pan heats up, place one leaf in the pan and lightly press it for a second. If the pan is not big enough to accommodate the entire leaf, you might have to move the leaf around on the pan. The heat will soften the leaf, which will make wrapping easy without tearing. Turn off the heat once you are done softening all the leaves.

To wrap the fish, place one banana leaf on a clean surface. Spoon 1 tablespoon (15 g) of the kashundi yogurt mixture in the center and place 1 hilsa fillet on top. Place 1 green chilli, sliced in half lengthwise, on top of the fillet. Fold one side of the leaf over the fish, then fold the opposite side of the leaf over the fish to cover. Then fold the remaining two sides over the top and seal the package using a toothpick or tie it using baking twine. Follow the same process to wrap the rest of the fillets.

Place the same pan that we used earlier back over medium-low heat and add the remaining 1 tablespoon (15 ml) of mustard oil. When the oil is hot, place the wrapped parcels in the pan and cover the pan. Cook for 5 minutes. Flip the parcels over and cook for 3 more minutes.

This is best served immediately with steamed rice on the side. You could also add more mustard oil while serving for the extra pungent taste.

Daab Chingri

(Shrimp Cooked in Tender Coconut)

Serves 2

This is a very interesting and unique dish because shrimp are cooked inside a tender coconut. The soft cream from the coconut, subtly sweet coconut water, fresh green chillies and mustard paste create a very interesting flavor combination. When served in those tender coconuts, it also makes a great centerpiece for parties.

1 lb (454 g) medium-size shrimp

2 medium-size tender coconuts

3 Indian green chillies, sliced in half, divided

1 tbsp (15 ml) mustard oil, divided

½ tsp nigella seeds

1 tbsp (10 g) grated garlic

1 small red onion, finely chopped

1 tsp salt, divided

½ tsp ground turmeric, divided

3 tbsp (47 g) shorshe baata (page 11)

Fresh cilantro leaves, for garnish

If you enjoy the shrimp head and shell, leave them on; otherwise, peel the shrimp and remove the head. To clean the shrimp, use a sharp knife to slit the back of the shrimp from end to end. Look for the black vein and remove it carefully. If you pull it gently, it will come out easily. Discard it. Once all the shrimp are clean, set aside.

Using a sharp knife, cut the top of the tender coconut to make a 3-inch (8-cm) wide opening. Pour the coconut water into a glass and, using a spoon, scrape off all the creamy flesh from inside. Slightly trim the bottom of the tender coconut so you can make it sit still.

Place the tender coconut flesh, 1 green chilli and 2 tablespoons (30 ml) of the coconut water in a blender and blend to a smooth paste. Set aside.

Next, place a pan over medium-high heat and add 1 teaspoon of the mustard oil. Add the nigella seeds and once the seeds start to sizzle, lower the heat to medium and let the seeds sizzle for a couple of seconds.

Add the grated garlic and finely chopped onion to the pan. Sprinkle with ½ teaspoon of the salt and ¼ teaspoon of the turmeric. Stir and cook for 3 minutes.

Remove from the heat and transfer to a mixing bowl along with the coconut paste, shrimp, *shorshe baata*, remaining ½ teaspoon of salt, remaining ¼ teaspoon of turmeric, remaining 2 teaspoons (10 ml) of mustard oil and remaining 2 green chillies. Stir and allow the shrimp to marinate for 15 minutes.

Preheat the oven to 375°F (191°C).

Divide the marinated shrimp and the spices between the two coconuts. Seal the top by wrapping tightly with aluminum foil. Place on a baking sheet and bake for 20 minutes.

Remove the coconuts from the oven, remove the foil (careful: the steam will be hot!), garnish with fresh cilantro leaves and serve immediately.

Lau Chingri

(Stir-Fried Bottle Gourd and Shrimp)

Serves 4

Because of the high water content in bottle gourd, this vegetable is used a lot during peak summer months. It's great for stomach ailments and is light on the digestive system. The vegetable can taste quite bland on its own, but add an earthy spice mix, tender shrimp and a handful of fresh cilantro, and it turns into a delicious dish.

1 potato (185 g/6.5 oz)

11 oz (300 g) headless, peeled shrimp

1 tsp salt, divided

1 tsp ground turmeric, divided

1 bottle gourd (700 g/1.5 lb)

1 tbsp (15 ml) oil, divided

1 bay leaf

1 tsp paanch phoron (page 11)

½ tsp sugar

½ tsp ground cumin

3 green chillies, sliced in half

¼ cup (12 g) finely chopped fresh cilantro

Peel the potato and cut it into ½-inch (1-cm) chunks. Set aside.

Depending on the size of the shrimp, you could leave them whole or cut into bite-size pieces. Place the shrimp in a bowl. Sprinkle with ¼ teaspoon of the salt and ½ teaspoon of the turmeric. Stir and set aside.

Trim the ends of the bottle gourd. Using a peeler, peel the skin. Slice the bottle gourd into ½-inch (1-cm) disks. Stack a few of the disks and cut into ¼-inch (0.5-cm) slices. If the slices are too long, then slice them in half. Set aside.

Place a heavy-bottomed saucepan over medium heat and add ½ teaspoon of oil. When the oil heats up, add the shrimp and fry for a couple of minutes. Transfer the shrimp to a bowl and set aside.

Heat the remaining 2½ teaspoons (12 ml) of oil in the same pan and add the bay leaf and *paanch phoron*. After a few seconds, add the diced potatoes and sprinkle with ¼ teaspoon of the salt. Cook for 4 minutes, stirring a couple of times.

Add the sliced bottle gourd, sugar, remaining ½ teaspoon of salt, remaining ½ teaspoon of turmeric and ground cumin and stir. Cover the pan and allow to cook for 10 minutes, stirring once in between.

After 10 minutes, add the fried shrimp and green chillies, stir and cook for 1 minute. Then add the finely chopped cilantro, stir and it's ready to serve.

Robibar Er Murgi Jhol

(Sunday Chicken Curry)

Serves 4

While there are several ways to eat chicken curry, this version of one-pot, flavor-packed chicken curry is often prepared by my Baba for Sunday lunch. A weekend without chicken curry feels incomplete, and on Sundays, Ma takes a break from cooking while Baba puts on his chef's hat and prepares this super-easy, mildly spiced dish. Ladled onto hot rice with a sprinkle of freshly squeezed lemon juice, it's an all-time comfort food.

1 lb (500 g) bite-size chicken pieces, mix of bone-in and boneless, without skin

1 tsp ground cumin

1 tsp ground coriander

1 tsp chilli powder

1 tbsp (15 ml) lemon juice

1 tbsp (15 g) salt, divided

1 potato

1 red onion

2 tbsp (30 ml) oil, divided

1 tsp ground turmeric, divided

1 tsp sugar

3 green cardamom pods

2 cloves

2 bay leaves

1-inch (3-cm) cinnamon stick

1 tbsp (10 g) grated garlic

1 tbsp (8 g) grated ginger

1 cup (237 ml) water

3 green chillies

1 tsp gorom moshla (page 11)

Fresh cilantro leaves, for garnish

Lime wedges

Put the chicken pieces in a big mixing bowl. Add the cumin, coriander, chilli powder, lemon juice and 1 teaspoon of the salt. Massage with your hands so the spices coat the pieces evenly. Cover the bowl and allow the chicken to marinate for a minimum of 4 hours. Letting it marinate overnight would make the flavor better.

Peel the potato and cut it into quarters. Set aside. Peel the onion. Slice three-fourths of the onion into thin slices and grate the remaining one-fourth of the onion.

When ready to prepare the chicken curry, place a heavy-bottomed saucepan over medium-high heat and add 1 tablespoon (15 ml) of the oil. When the oil heats up, add the potato. Sprinkle with ½ teaspoon of the salt and ½ teaspoon of the turmeric. Stir and fry the potato until mildly golden in color, about 3 minutes. Remove the potato from the pan to a separate bowl and set aside.

To the same pan, add the remaining 1 tablespoon (15 ml) of oil and the sugar. Allow the sugar to caramelize for a few seconds and then add the green cardamom, cloves, bay leaves and cinnamon stick. Allow them to sizzle for a few seconds, then add the garlic, ginger and grated onion. Stir and cook for 5 minutes, then add the sliced onion. Sprinkle with the remaining 1½ teaspoons (8 g) of salt and the remaining ½ teaspoon of turmeric. Stir and allow the onion to cook and turn golden brown in color, about 5 minutes.

Add the marinated chicken, stir to combine everything evenly and cook for 5 minutes. After 5 minutes, add the fried potatoes, water and green chillies and cook for 15 minutes or until the chicken is cooked through.

Finally, sprinkle with the *gorom moshla*, stir and check for salt at this point. Add any if required. Cook for 2 more minutes and turn off the heat.

Garnish with fresh cilantro leaves, squeeze fresh lime juice on top and serve warm.

Patla Murgi Jhol

(Gently Spiced Chicken Stew)

Serves 4

This is a very subtly spiced chicken stew. It's perfect for days when you are under the weather. The stew is extremely light and not spicy. The gravy is not thick but light like broth. Baba always adds a few chunks of tiny red onions for their subtle sweetness. I love to enjoy this chicken stew in a bowl with less rice and more broth.

Key Notes: In India, the size of the onions is very tiny as compared to what you get in the United States, so I often replace them with shallots. Adding a few tiny whole shallots adds a nice texture and sweetness to the stew, but it's optional and can easily be skipped.

1.8 lb (800 g) bone-in skinless chicken pieces

2 tsp (10 g) salt, divided

¼ tsp chilli powder

½ tsp ground coriander

1 tsp ground cumin

1 small onion (113 g/4 oz)

4 cloves garlic

4 shallots

2 potatoes (150 g/5.3 oz)

2 tbsp (30 ml) oil, divided

½ tsp ground turmeric, divided

2 bay leaves

1 tbsp (8 g) grated ginger

½ tsp sugar

2 cups (473 ml) water

¼ cup (12 g) finely chopped fresh cilantro

In a bowl, combine the chicken pieces with 1 teaspoon of the salt, chilli powder, coriander and cumin. Massage the spices into the chicken with your hands and let it marinate for 4 hours minimum or overnight for best flavor.

Using a food processor or a sharp knife, finely chop the onion and garlic. Also peel the shallots and set aside. Peel the potatoes and cut each into quarters.

Heat 1 tablespoon (15 ml) of the oil in a heavy-bottomed pan over medium-high heat. Add the potato quarters and sprinkle with ½ teaspoon of salt and ¼ teaspoon of the turmeric. Fry the potatoes for 4 minutes, stirring often. Remove the potatoes from the pan and set aside in a bowl.

In the same heavy-bottomed pan, add the remaining 1 tablespoon (15 ml) of oil and the bay leaves and allow it to flavor for 2 seconds. Add the chopped onion, garlic, ginger, remaining ½ teaspoon of salt, remaining ¼ teaspoon of turmeric and the sugar; stir. Allow the onion to soften for 4 minutes.

Now add the marinated chicken, stir and let the chicken cook for 5 minutes, stirring once. Add the fried potatoes and water, stir and bring the water to a boil. Then lower the heat to medium, cover the pan and allow it to cook for 15 minutes. Remove the lid, stir and add the shallots. Cook for another 5 minutes. Taste for salt and add any if required. Finally, garnish with the cilantro and it's ready to serve.

Kosha Mangsho

(Spiced Slow-Cooked Mutton)

Serves 4

Arvind didn't grow up eating mutton and he doesn't like the flavor of lamb. So, when I was preparing this dish for him for the first time, I kept my fingers crossed. I called Ma, wrote down the recipe in as much detail as I could, picked the best fresh mutton pieces I could find and slow cooked it for the best flavor. When we sat down for dinner, Arvind not only went for a second serving, but he also declared that *kosha mangsho* is his new favorite Bengali dish. That is the magic of this spiced slow-cooked mutton stew.

1½ tbsp (22 ml) oil
(preferably mustard oil)

½ tsp sugar

2 bay leaves

4 green cardamom pods, smashed

4 cloves

1 tbsp (8 g) grated ginger

1 tbsp (10 g) grated garlic

1 red onion, finely chopped

1 tsp salt, divided

1 tomato, grated

½ tsp ground turmeric

1 tsp ground cumin

1 tsp Indian red chilli powder

½ tsp ground coriander

1 lb (454 g) goat/mutton meat (bone-in and boneless mixed), cut into 1½-inch (4-cm) cubes

1 tbsp (14 g) ghee (clarified butter)

2 Indian green chillies, sliced in half

½ tbsp gorom moshla (page 11)

Finely chopped cilantro leaves, for garnish

Lime wedges

Place a heavy-bottomed wok or saucepan over medium-high heat. Add the oil and once the oil heats up, sprinkle in the sugar. Allow the sugar to caramelize for a few seconds and then add the bay leaves, cardamom and cloves. Let them sizzle for a few seconds.

Next, add the ginger, garlic and onion. Sprinkle with ½ teaspoon of the salt and stir. Allow the onion to turn light golden in color, about 3 minutes.

Add the tomato, turmeric, cumin, chilli powder and coriander. Stir. Cook for 2 minutes. Add the mutton pieces and the remaining ½ teaspoon of salt, give it a stir and turn down the heat to medium-low. Cover the pan/wok with a tight-fitting lid and cook for 40 minutes. Stir every now and then to make sure the spices and the mutton pieces don't stick to the bottom of the pan. Sprinkle in a little water if that happens and stir.

Once the mutton is cooked and falls off the bones, check for salt and add any if required. Add the ghee, green chillies and gorom moshla. Stir and allow it to cook for 5 more minutes, and then turn off the heat.

Sprinkle with some chopped fresh cilantro and squeeze fresh lime juice on top just before serving.

Dim Omelet Er Jhol

(Fluffy Omelet in Tomato Gravy)

Serves 4 or 5

This is a quintessential Bengali egg curry! I could eat eggs for breakfast, lunch and dinner, if given a choice. Boiled egg curries are my go-to meal because they're just so quick to prepare. But making an egg omelet curry is much faster because you save time on boiling the eggs. When the omelet is cooked in tomato gravy, it gets soft and pillowy. Paired with *ruti* (page 14) or *bhaat* (page 12), it's a meal that is very comforting.

5 eggs

1½ tsp (8 g) salt, divided

1 potato (5.3 oz/150 g)

1 red onion (8 oz/226 g)

3 tbsp (45 ml) oil, divided

1 tsp ground turmeric, divided

1 tsp cumin seeds

½ tsp sugar

1 tbsp (15 g) tomato paste

½ tsp ground cumin

½ tsp ground coriander

¼ tsp Indian red chilli powder

1 tbsp plus ½ cup (133 ml) water, divided

2 Indian green chillies, slit in half

Fresh cilantro, for garnish

Lemon wedges (optional)

Crack the eggs into a bowl, add ¼ teaspoon of the salt and whisk until smooth. Peel the potato and cut it in half lengthwise, then cut each half into 3 or 4 wedges. Peel the onion and cut it in half and then finely chop each half.

Place a 9-inch (23-cm) skillet over medium heat and, when hot, add 1 tablespoon (15 ml) of the oil. Swirl the pan to spread the oil around and then pour in the whisked eggs. Swirl the pan to spread it evenly. Cook for 2 minutes or until the edges of the omelet are set and the center is almost set too. Using a spatula, lift one side of the omelet and fold it halfway over, pressing the top with the spatula. Then lift the edge again and give one more fold to reach the other edge of the omelet. Turn off the heat, remove the omelet from the pan and place it on a chopping board. When it is cool enough to handle, cut the omelet into 4 or 5 equal portions. Set aside.

Turn the heat back on to medium-high and add 1 tablespoon (15 ml) of oil to the same pan. When the pan is hot, add the potato wedges, sprinkle with ¼ teaspoon of salt and ½ teaspoon of the turmeric and stir. Cook for 5 minutes, tossing every now and then. Transfer the potatoes to a bowl and set aside.

To the same pan add the remaining 1 tablespoon (15 ml) of oil and drop in the cumin seeds. Once it sizzles, drop the finely chopped onion, the remaining 1 teaspoon of salt, the remaining ½ teaspoon of turmeric and the sugar and stir. Cook for 2 minutes or until the onion turns mildly golden brown. Add the tomato paste and stir to combine. Next, combine the ground cumin, ground coriander and chilli powder and 1 tablespoon (15 ml) of the water in a bowl. Stir to blend and pour the mixture into the pan. Stir and cook for 5 minutes or until the oil starts to release from the sides.

Add the remaining ½ cup (118 ml) of water and the green chillies and stir. Crank up the heat, bring the water to a boil and add the fried potatoes. Once it starts to boil, turn the heat down to medium, cover the pan and cook for 5 minutes or until the potatoes are tender. Check for salt at this stage and add any if required. If you prefer more gravy, add more water. Nestle the sliced omelets into the gravy and cook for a couple more minutes. Garnish with fresh cilantro leaves, squeeze some lemon juice on top and serve warm.

Dim Papad Er Dalna

(Boiled Eggs and Papadum Stew)

Serves 4

In this dish, boiled eggs are cooked in spiced gravy and at the end, a few roasted papadum are added. This is one of my aunt's recipes. She prepares this dish with loads of vegetables or with boiled eggs. Adding roasted papadum instead of raw ones lends a nice smoky flavor to the stew. It's a quick, easy and hearty stew.

4 hard-boiled eggs

1 tsp salt, divided

1 tsp turmeric, divided

1 tsp Indian chilli powder, divided

1 tsp grated garlic

½ tbsp (4 g) grated ginger

1 medium red onion, finely chopped

3 (3-inch [7.5-cm] diameter) papadum

3 tbsp (45 ml) oil, divided

1 tsp sugar

1 tsp ground cumin

1 tsp ground coriander

1 tbsp plus ½ cup (133 ml) water, divided

1 Indian green chilli, sliced in half

1 tomato, finely chopped

Using a sharp knife, score the boiled eggs gently all around. Place the sliced egg in a small mixing bowl. Sprinkle with ½ teaspoon of the salt, ½ teaspoon of the turmeric and ½ teaspoon of the chilli powder. Stir gently.

In another bowl, combine the garlic, ginger and onion. Set aside.

Place a pan over medium-high heat and dry roast the papadum. Place one papadum at a time in the pan, press the papadum down with a spatula for 2 seconds and then turn it over, press it again with the spatula and roast for 2 more seconds. Repeat the process with the rest of the papadum and set aside on a plate.

Place a heavy-bottomed saucepan or a wok over medium heat and add 1 tablespoon (15 ml) of the oil. When the oil is hot, add the eggs and fry for 1 minute, tossing around gently. Remove the eggs from the pan and place in a separate bowl.

Heat the remaining 2 tablespoons (30 ml) of oil in the same saucepan and add the garlic, ginger and onion mixture. Sprinkle with the sugar, remaining ½ teaspoon of salt and remaining ½ teaspoon of turmeric, stir to combine and cook for 5 minutes, stirring every now and then. The onion mixture will cook down and turn a light brown shade.

In a small bowl, combine the cumin, coriander, remaining ½ teaspoon of chilli powder and 1 tablespoon (15 ml) of the water. Stir and pour it into the saucepan. Stir, add the green chilli and cook for 2 minutes. Add the finely chopped tomato and cook for 5 more minutes or until the oil starts to release from the edges.

Place the fried boiled eggs in the saucepan and add the remaining ½ cup (118 ml) of water. Stir slowly and crank up the heat to high. Once the water starts boiling, lower the heat to medium and cook for 3 minutes. Check for salt and add any if required.

Turn off the heat, break the roasted papadum roughly into big bite-size pieces and add them to the saucepan. Cover the saucepan for 3 minutes. The hot steam will soften the papadum. After 3 minutes, remove the lid, and stir to mix the softened papadum evenly with the gravy. Serve warm.

Smack Your Palate

We all need a little bit of zest in our life to make it exciting every now and then. The same holds true for our palate, especially when you have so much to indulge in. A palate cleanser every now and then is always welcoming. It helps ready your taste buds for the next course.

In this chapter, I share a few of the chutney and pickle recipes that I have learned from Ma. Summer was always about making multiple batches of homemade pickles, some spicy and some sweet. Prepared with seasonal fruits and vegetables, chutneys in Bengali cuisine are always served right at the end of the meal.

Bengalis are fond of fish and most summer lunches include a tangy stew prepared with tiny freshwater fish. The pungent mustard sauce *kashundi* is very popularly used to prepare meals and served as a dip.

Fulkopir Aachar

(Indian Spiced Cauliflower Pickle)

Makes 2 cups (459 g)

Summer is always about making multiple batches of spicy pickles. Growing up, we never bought pickles; they were always homemade. Sometimes we used vegetables and other times fruits. The cauliflower pickle has always been a favorite and it makes a great condiment to serve along with several different dishes.

½ head cauliflower

3 tbsp (45 ml) mustard oil

2 bay leaves

1 tbsp (6 g) paanch phoron (page 11)

2 Indian dried red chillies

1 tsp salt

½ tsp ground turmeric

½ tbsp (6 g) sugar

1 tsp ground coriander

1 tsp Indian red chilli powder

¼ cup (59 ml) white vinegar

Cut the cauliflower into bite-size florets and place them in a colander. Wash the florets under running water and then leave them in the colander for a couple of hours or until the cauliflower is completely dried.

When you are ready to make the pickle, heat the mustard oil in a deep, heavy-bottomed pan over medium heat. Add the bay leaves, *paanch phoron* and Indian dried red chillies. After a few seconds, the spices will start to sizzle.

Add the cauliflower florets and sprinkle with the salt, turmeric and sugar. Stir and cover the pan for 5 minutes.

Remove the lid after 5 minutes and sprinkle with the coriander and Indian red chilli powder. Stir and cover the pan once again for 2 minutes. The florets should be softened by now; if not, then stir and cover it again and cook until the cauliflower is tender.

Add the vinegar and cook for 1 more minute. Check for salt and add any if required. If you would prefer a spicier pickle, add more Indian red chilli powder and cook for 1 minute longer.

Allow the pickle to cool completely and then store in a clean, airtight glass jar in the refrigerator.

Kashundi

(Green Mango Mustard Sauce)

Makes 2 cups (473 ml)

My aunt makes a big batch of this fiery and pungent sauce every year. As a kid, I could never embrace the flavor, but now it's a totally different story. Ever since I tried her recipe, I've been hooked. Now I also make it every summer. The sauce stays good for an entire year if kept in a clean, airtight glass jar. I always store it in multiple mason jars and keep it in the freezer until needed.

Key Notes: Mustard seed is a tricky ingredient. If you grind it for too long, it will turn from pungent to inedibly bitter. Another key element for this sauce is the mustard oil. It's the oil that makes the sauce pungent. It's important to coat the entire sauce in mustard oil and let it rest for a few hours. I have realized that after a couple of days, the taste gets much better, bringing out the beautiful balance of flavors: a hint of sour, the spiciness of mustard seed, the heat of green chillies and that super pungency of raw mustard oil.

½ cup (76 g) black mustard seeds

¼ cup (38 g) yellow mustard seeds

3 sour green mangoes

4 or 5 green chillies, roughly chopped

1 tbsp (8 g) ground turmeric

Salt to taste

½ cup (118 ml) white vinegar

1 cup (237 ml) mustard oil, divided

Grind the mustard seeds in a spice grinder or mortar and pestle to a coarse consistency.

Peel the mangoes and grind the pulp and chopped green chillies to a paste.

In a medium saucepan, combine the mango paste, ground mustard seeds, turmeric and salt to taste. Add the vinegar and ½ cup (118 ml) of the mustard oil. Stir and cook for just 2 minutes. Taste for salt.

Turn off the heat, add the remaining ½ cup (118 ml) of mustard oil, mix and let it rest for a couple of hours. Once it comes to room temperature, pour it into an airtight bottle and keep it in the refrigerator. The spice and pungency get better after a couple of days.

Kacha Aam Makha

(Green Mango with Kashundi Sauce)

Makes 2 cups (473 ml)

Wedges of green mango rubbed with Indian red chilli powder and salt is a favorite summer snack in India. This *aam makha* is similar to that, except the green mango is grated and then mixed with pungent *kashundi* sauce. This is a quintessential afternoon snack for Bengalis. It also makes a great condiment for vegetable or chicken wraps.

2 cups (180 g) grated green mango

3 tbsp (46 g) kashundi (page 116)

1 tsp sugar, plus more if the green mango is too tart

½ tsp salt

½ tsp cumin seeds

¼ cup (12 g) finely chopped fresh cilantro

Freshly squeezed lime juice (optional)

Put everything in a bowl and stir. Taste for salt and sugar. Add any, if required. Serve immediately.

Anarosh Till Chutney

(Pineapple Sesame Seed Chutney)

Serves 2

It's typical to end a Bengali meal with chutney. The chutneys are always prepared with seasonal fruits and vegetables. I prepared this dish for the first time when I was testing recipes for the book. Ma explained the recipe over a phone call. The dish turned out so good that I kept making it again and again. Creamy sesame seed paste blends beautifully with the sweet and sour pineapple chunks. Served in a bowl at the end of the meal, or served with rice or with some savory crackers, this chutney will surely wake up your palate.

2 tbsp (20 g) white sesame seeds, plus a little extra to add as garnish at the end

5 tbsp (74 ml) water, divided

1 tsp oil

1 tsp paanch phoron (page 11)

2 bay leaves

1 Indian dried red chilli

15 oz (432 g) diced pineapple cubes

½ tsp salt

¼ tsp tumeric

1 tbsp (12 g) sugar

Soak the white sesame seeds in 2 tablespoons (30 ml) of the water for 30 minutes. Then, using a mortar and pestle or a small blender, grind it to a paste. Set aside.

Place a heavy-bottomed pan over medium heat and add the oil. When the oil heats up, add the paanch phoron, bay leaves and dried Indian red chilli. Allow them to sizzle for a few seconds, then add the diced pineapple. Sprinkle with the salt, tumeric and sugar. Stir and cook for 5 minutes.

Add the sesame paste and remaining 3 tablespoons (45 ml) of water. Cook for 2 more minutes, check for salt and sugar and add any if required. Sprinkle sesame seeds on top as garnish.

The chutney tastes good warm or at room temperature.

Kacha Aam Er Chutney

(Green Mango Sweet and Sour Chutney)

Serves 4

This is my brother's favorite chutney. He eats tart fruits like candy, and prefers tart chutney over the sweet variety. So when Ma prepares this chutney, she always takes out his portion and adds more sugar to make it sweeter. This sweet and tart chutney to finish the meal will tickle your taste buds. Wedges of green mango are cooked until tender with subtle spices and then finished with some crushed fennel seed for that refreshing flavor. Depending on how sour the raw mangoes are, you will have to adjust the quantity of the sugar accordingly.

1 green mango

3 tbsp (36 g) sugar, divided

1 tsp salt

½ tsp Indian chilli powder

1 tsp fennel seeds, divided

1 tsp oil

1 tsp black mustard seeds

2 Indian dried red chillies

½ cup (118 ml) water

Peel the mango and slice the pulp into thin wedges and discard the pit. Place the wedges in a bowl and sprinkle with 1 tablespoon (12 g) of the sugar, the salt and the chilli powder. Massage the spices into the mango and set aside.

Place a pan or wok over medium heat. Once it's hot, add ½ teaspoon of the fennel seeds and dry roast for a few seconds. Transfer the fennel seeds to a mortar and pestle and crush to a coarse texture. Set aside.

Place a pan over medium heat and add the oil. Once it heats up, add the mustard seeds, dried red chillies and remaining ½ teaspoon of fennel seeds. Allow the spices to sizzle for a few seconds and then add the mango slices. Spread out the slices in the pan and cook for 2 minutes. The sugar will start to caramelize and coat the mango slices. Stir and cook for 2 more minutes.

Add the remaining 2 tablespoons (24 g) of sugar and the water. Bring the water to a boil and cook for 5 minutes or until the mango slices are almost soft. Taste for salt and sugar at this point. Add any if required.

Finally, sprinkle the crushed roasted fennel seeds on top and cook for 2 more minutes. Turn off the heat and allow the chutney to come to room temperature before you serve.

Tomato Khejur Er Chutney

(Tomato and Date Chutney)

Serves 4

This is my all-time favorite chutney and I also got Arvind to fall in love with it. If there was mutton on the menu, Ma would always prepare this chutney for me. The pairing of rich meat curry with this sweet tomato chutney is like a marriage made in heaven. Every time I make this chutney, we end up eating more and there is barely any left over.

4 tomatoes

4.75 oz (134 g) pitted soft dates

1 tsp fennel seeds, divided

1 tsp oil

1 tsp black mustard seeds

2 Indian dried red chillies

3 tbsp (36 g) sugar

½ tsp salt

Slice each tomato in half and slice each half into thin wedges. Cut the dates in half lengthwise.

Place a small pan over medium-high heat. When the pan heats up, add ½ teaspoon of the fennel seeds and dry roast for a minute. Shake the pan as you dry roast to keep the seeds from burning. Transfer the seeds to a mortar and pestle, allow them to cool off a bit and then crush it to a fine powder. Set aside.

Place a deep saucepan over medium heat and add the oil. When the oil heats up, add the remaining ½ teaspoon of fennel seeds, the mustard seeds and the dried red chillies. Once the seeds start to sizzle, add the sliced tomato and sprinkle with the sugar and salt. Stir and cook for 5 minutes.

Add the sliced dates, stir and cook for 5 more minutes. Taste for salt and sugar. Add any if required. Add the crushed fennel seeds. Give it a final stir. Turn off the heat and it's ready to serve.

Tangra Maach Er Tok

(Tiny Fish Tangy Stew)

Serves 4

On warm summer days, this soulful fish stew gets prepared quite often, especially for lunch. It's aromatic, very mildly spiced and the tanginess helps sooth the tummy. The souring agent used here is green raw mango, but it can also be prepared with tamarind. However, the green mango adds an extra depth of flavor.

1 lb (500 g) tangra maach (small catfish)

1 tsp salt, divided

1 tsp ground turmeric, divided

1 green mango

¼ cup (59 ml) oil

1 tsp black mustard seeds

3 Indian green chillies, sliced in half

1 tsp sugar

½ cup (118 ml) water

2 tbsp (6 g) finely chopped cilantro

Place the fish in a bowl and sprinkle with ½ teaspoon of the salt and ½ teaspoon of the turmeric. Massage the spices into the fish and let it marinate for 30 minutes.

Peel the mango, slice the pulp into thin wedges and discard the pit.

Place a nonstick heavy-bottomed pan over medium-high heat and add the oil. Place a kitchen towel on a plate and keep it ready. Once the oil heats up, very carefully add the marinated fish, without overcrowding the pan. They will start to sizzle. Fry for 3 minutes. Using a slotted spoon, transfer the fried fish to the kitchen towel to drain.

Remove the excess oil from the pan leaving 1 teaspoon. Carefully (as it will splatter) add the black mustard seeds and green chillies. After a couple of seconds, add the mango wedges and sprinkle with the remaining ½ teaspoon of salt and remaining ½ teaspoon of turmeric. Give it a stir and sprinkle with the sugar. Cook the mango wedges for 5 minutes or until they are softened but still retain their shape.

Add the water and bring it to a boil. Then add the fried fish back to the pan and cook for 2 minutes. Check for salt and add any if required. If it's too sour, add more sugar to balance it out.

Finally, sprinkle with the finely chopped cilantro and serve warm or at room temperature.

Sweet Tooth

I didn't have a huge sweet tooth while growing up. I just had a few favorites in the wide range of delectable *mishti* (sweets) that Bengali cuisine has to offer. My friends used to say that I shouldn't even call myself a Bengali because I couldn't finish even one *roshogolla* (cheese dumpling), whereas they could gulp one after another. It was during my pregnancy that the craving for sweets started and it hasn't stopped since. I guess I have become a true Bengali after all.

Most Bengali desserts are milk-based, prepared either with *chaana* (fresh cheese) or *kheer* (solid milk) or dipped in cream. *Pitha* is a category of sweets that is unique to eastern India. It is mostly prepared with rice flour combined with either white or wheat flour. Coconut and jaggery are used to flavor these pithas.

While deciding on the list of desserts for this section, I picked all the classics that Ma has taught me over the years.

Please note that sweet treats that call for chaana (page 13) cannot be replaced with store-bought paneer. The texture is different and unless you use fresh chaana, you will not get the expected soft consistency for these sweets.

Chaana Payesh

(Fresh Cheese Dumplings in Cream)

Makes 12 dumplings

This is my *dida*'s (my mom's mom) specialty. She used to prepare this dessert whenever she didn't have much time but needed a sweet treat at the end of the meal. Fresh cheese dumplings are cooked in flavored milk until they turn soft and spongy. You definitely want to make the *chaana* fresh for the best texture of the dumplings.

1½ cups (344 g) chaana (page 13)

1 cup (237 ml) whole milk

2 cups (473 ml) heavy cream

5 green cardamom pods

2 bay leaves

5 tbsp (60 g) sugar

10 to 12 raisins

Sliced pistachios, for garnish

Place the chaana on a flat plate or chopping board, spread it out and knead it by hand for 10 minutes. Don't use too much pressure; just lightly press it with the heels of your palm and then gather the chaana and press again. After 10 minutes, you will notice that your hand feels mildly oily and the chaana dough will feel extremely soft but still hold its shape.

Divide the chaana dough into 12 portions and roll each one in your palms to form a soft ball. Make sure there are no cracks. Then slightly press it to form a disk. Shape all the dumplings the same way.

Place a wide, heavy-bottomed saucepan over medium-high heat and add the milk, heavy cream, cardamom, bay leaves and sugar. Bring it to a boil, stirring every now and then to prevent the milk from getting burned at the bottom of the pan. Once it comes to a boil, reduce the heat to medium and let it simmer for 10 minutes, again stirring occasionally.

After 10 minutes, add the shaped dumplings and let them simmer for 15 minutes, stirring occasionally. The dumplings will double in size as they cook, so they need enough space. Depending on how big your pan is, you may need to do this in batches. Finally, add the raisins, remove from the heat and let the *chaana payesh* cool to room temperature.

Spoon out some dumplings and flavored milk among bowls, sprinkle with some sliced pistachios and serve at room temperature.

Choshi Payesh

(Rice Flour Vermicelli Sweet Pudding)

Serves 4

Preparing this pudding was a ritual every Bengali New Year, especially at my grandparents' house. We kids would roll the vermicelli while our grandma would sit by the earthen stove simmering away a huge brass wok of milk. These days, I prepare this vermicelli with the help of my son. This pudding takes longer to prepare, but in the end, it all feels worth the work. Note that the vermicelli has to be prepared the day before.

FOR THE VERMICELLI

¾ cup (177 ml) water

1 cup (151 g) rice flour

½ tsp salt

FOR THE PUDDING

4 cups (946 ml) whole milk

1 bay leaf

3 green cardamom pods

1 cup (144 g) grated jaggery

2 tbsp (30 ml) water

Slivered pistachios, for garnish

To make the vermicelli, place a heavy-bottomed nonstick pan over medium-high heat. Add the water and bring it to a boil. Add the flour and salt, no need to stir at this point. Reduce the heat to medium-low and cover the pan. Cook for 3 minutes.

With a wooden spoon, mix the rice flour with the water to form pea-size crumbs. If it gets too dry to come together, then sprinkle with a little warm water and continue forming the dough. Similarly, if it gets too watery, add extra flour. Once the dough comes together, transfer it to a cutting board and knead it to a smooth dough while the mixture is still warm. Cover the dough with a damp kitchen towel. It's important to cover the dough, as it gets dry very quickly.

Sprinkle a little flour on a clean chopping board. Divide the dough into 4 portions. Cover 3 portions with the damp kitchen towel and roll one portion into a log. Cut the log into 5 or 6 portions. Roll each portion into thin strings. Pinch a tiny portion from the string and roll it into vermicelli, rubbing it in your hands, as shown in the photos. Place the vermicelli on a separate plate or board and dust some more flour on top, just to keep them from sticking to one another. Continue working with the rest of the dough the same way. Once the vermicelli is prepared, let it rest overnight.

To make the pudding, add the milk to a heavy-bottomed saucepan, then add the bay leaf and cardamom and bring to a boil over medium-high heat. Lower the heat to medium and let it simmer for 10 minutes, stirring every now and then. After 10 minutes, add half of the vermicelli, stir, cook for a few seconds and then add the rest of the vermicelli. Stir and cook over medium heat for 10 to 15 minutes. The timing will depend a lot on the size of the noodles you prepared. Keep checking every 5 minutes by picking out one strand and biting into it.

While the vermicelli cooks, melt the jaggery and water in a pan over medium heat. Once the vermicelli is cooked through, turn down the heat to low and allow the pudding to cool down a little bit. Then add the melted jaggery and stir. If you add melted jaggery to very hot milk, sometimes it can curdle, spoiling the entire dish. Turn the heat back to medium and cook for a couple of minutes. Garnish the pudding with slivered pistachios and serve warm or cold.

Malai Chum Chum

(Juicy Cheese Dumplings in Saffron Cream Sauce)

Makes 12 dumplings

Another very popular dessert is *malai chum chum*. These dumplings are velvety and spongy and melt in your mouth. You definitely want to make a lot because it's hard to stop at just one.

Key Notes: Solid milk is sold in most Indian stores in the frozen section.

FOR THE FILLING AND SAUCE

¼ cup (59 ml) milk

Pinch of saffron threads

1 cup (116 g) grated solid milk, divided

3 tbsp (24 g) powdered sugar, divided

½ tsp ground cardamom

¼ cup (59 ml) heavy cream

FOR THE CHEESE DUMPLINGS

1 cup (230 g) chaana (page 13)

4 cups (946 ml) water

2 cups (383 g) granulated sugar

5 green cardamom pods, crushed

Slivered almonds for garnish

Add the milk and saffron to a small bowl, stir to combine and set aside.

To make the dumplings, spread the chaana and, using your hands, knead it for 10 minutes. Don't use too much pressure; just lightly press it with the heels of your palms and then gather the chaana and press again. After 10 minutes, you will notice that your hands feel mildly oily and the chaana dough will feel extremely soft but still hold its shape. Divide the chaana dough into 12 portions. Roll each portion into a 1-inch (3-cm) long oblong shape. Make sure there are no cracks. Once you are done shaping the dumplings, set them aside to be boiled in hot syrup.

Place a deep, 9-inch (23-cm) saucepan over high heat. Add the water, granulated sugar and green cardamom and bring to a boil. Once the syrup starts to a boil, turn the heat down to medium-high and continue boiling for 15 minutes. After 15 minutes, turn the heat down to medium and add the prepared chaana dumplings. The dumplings will double in size as they boil, so they need enough space. Depending on how big your pan is, you may need to do this in batches.

Cover the pan and let the dumplings boil for 15 minutes. After 15 minutes, turn off the heat and let the dumplings rest in the syrup until cool enough to handle. Remove the dumplings from the syrup with a slotted spoon, gently press to squeeze out the excess syrup and place on a plate to be filled.

To prepare the filling, in a bowl, combine ½ cup (58 g) of the grated solid milk, 1 tablespoon (8 g) of the powdered sugar and the cardamom. Stir, and then add half of the reserved saffron milk and stir again. With a sharp knife, cut the cooked dumplings in half lengthwise. Using a butter knife, spread a little bit of the filling on one half of the dumpling and then place the other half on top, like a sandwich. Place it on a serving plate. Fill the rest of the sweet dumplings in the same way.

To prepare the sauce, place a small skillet or saucepan over medium heat. Add the heavy cream, the remaining ½ cup (58 g) of solid milk, the remaining 2 tablespoons (16 g) of powdered sugar and the remaining half of the saffron milk. Stir and cook for a minute to make a smooth sauce. Pour it on top of the filled dumplings. Sprinkle some slivered almonds on top and serve.

Roshogolla

(Juicy Cheese Dumplings in Light Sugar Syrup)

Makes 12 dumplings

These sweet syrup dumplings are every Bengali's favorite. It's a must for every gathering or celebration, big or small. On family gatherings, sometimes there would be fun competitions to see how many *roshogollas* one can gulp in one sitting. In Kolkata, no one prepares roshogolla at home because it's so readily available in every single sweet shop and there is at least one sweet shop in every lane. It's one of the easiest desserts to prepare but can be tricky at first. Once you get the hang of it, you will absolutely enjoy the whole process.

Key Note: This dessert cannot be prepared with store-bought *chaana*. The cheese has to be fresh or the roshogolla will not turn out spongy.

1 cup (230 g) chaana (page 13)

4 cups (946 ml) water

2 cups (383 g) sugar

5 green cardamom pods, crushed

Place the chaana on a flat plate or chopping board. Spread the chaana and, using your hands, knead it for 10 minutes. Don't use too much pressure; just lightly press it with the heels of your palms and then gather the chaana and press again. After 10 minutes, you will notice that your hands feel mildly oily and the chaana dough will feel extremely soft but still hold its shape.

Divide the chaana dough into 12 portions. Roll each portion to form a soft ball. Make sure there are no cracks. Once you are done making the balls, set them aside to be boiled in hot syrup.

Place a deep, 9-inch (23-cm) saucepan over high heat. Add the water, sugar and green cardamom and bring to a boil. Once the syrup starts to boil, turn the heat down to medium-high and continue boiling for 15 minutes.

After 15 minutes, turn the heat down to medium and add the prepared chaana dumplings. The dumplings will double in size as they boil, so they need enough space. Depending on how big your pan is, you may need to do this in batches.

Cover the pan and let the dumplings boil for 15 minutes. After 15 minutes, turn off the heat, remove the lid and let the roshogollas rest in the syrup until ready to serve.

Murir Mua

(Sweet Puffed Rice Balls)

Makes 20 balls

This is every child's favorite treat and now it is my son's favorite, too. Crunchy, airy puffed rice mixed with jaggery syrup is shaped into tiny balls that fit perfectly in their tiny palms. Ma always adds fennel seeds to the jaggery syrup and that gives it a lovely, refreshing aroma.

Key Note: Cooking the jaggery to a perfect consistency is very important, otherwise, the puffed rice won't hold together to form the balls.

1 tsp fennel seeds

9 oz (250 g) jaggery

3.5 oz (100 g) puffed rice

Place a pan over medium-high heat and add the fennel seeds. Dry roast the fennel for a few seconds, and then transfer it to a mortar and pestle. Pound it to a coarse powder and set aside.

Grate the jaggery block or shave it using a sharp knife.

Place a heavy-bottomed nonstick saucepan over medium heat. When the pan heats up, add the puffed rice and dry roast it for about 3 minutes, stirring every now and then. Once the puffed rice gets crunchy, transfer to a separate bowl.

Now add the grated jaggery to the same hot pan. Cook for about 4 minutes, stirring constantly. Have a small bowl filled with water ready. Add a tiny bit of the cooked jaggery to the bowl; if the shape holds and doesn't melt away, then your jaggery is ready. If not, continue cooking over medium heat, stirring constantly, until you get the right consistency.

Once the jaggery is cooked to the perfect consistency, add the crushed fennel seeds and stir. Then add the puffed rice and mix everything together so the jaggery syrup coats the puffed rice evenly. Transfer to a big bowl or plate.

You have to form the balls while the mixture is still warm. Place a bowl of cold water next to the plate of the jaggery-coated puffed rice. Dip your hands into the cold water, then take a small amount of the puffed rice and press it firmly with your palms to form a ball. Set aside. Continue making the rest of the *murir mua* the same way, dipping your hands into the bowl of water every now and then to prevent your hands from getting too sticky. You should get about 20 balls.

Murir mua will stay good for several weeks. You don't need to refrigerate them—just store in an airtight jar.

Malpua

(Sweet Fried Dumpling)

Makes 40 dumplings

Most people enjoy these sweet fried dumplings dipped in sugar syrup. I have always liked them puffed up and airy without the syrup. Paired with a cup of tea or warm milk, it was my favorite go-to dessert. Ma always prepares extra because somehow *malpuas* taste better the next day, with or without the syrup.

Key Notes: The batter needs to be prepared in advance and allowed to rest for 30 minutes for the best airy texture. If you don't like the malpuas airy and prefer the flat variety, omit the baking soda from the ingredients list.

FOR THE MALPUAS

1 tsp fennel seeds

2 cups (250 g) all-purpose flour

½ cup (88 g) fine semolina

½ cup (96 g) sugar

Tiny pinch of baking soda

½ cup (118 ml) milk

2 cups (473 ml) water

Oil, for deep-frying

FOR THE SYRUP (OPTIONAL)

2 cups (383 g) sugar

2 cups (473 ml) water

3 cloves

3 green cardamom pods

To make the malpuas, coarsely grind the fennel seeds in a mortar and pestle.

In a mixing bowl, whisk together the flour, semolina, sugar, crushed fennel seeds and baking soda. Add the milk and water and whisk the batter for 5 minutes to make it airy. You could also use an electric mixer. Cover the mixing bowl and let it sit for 30 minutes.

Place a deep, heavy-bottomed saucepan over medium heat and add the oil to reach a depth of 2 inches (5 cm). Layer a plate with a kitchen towel.

Once the oil reaches 300°F (149°C), whisk the batter once again. Take 2 tablespoons (30 ml) of the batter and slowly add it to the hot oil. Add as many dumplings as you can without overcrowding the pan. The malpuas will puff up and release from the bottom of the pan. Allow them to fry for about 5 minutes, tossing every now and then, until they turn golden brown in color. Using a slotted spoon, transfer the malpuas to the kitchen towel to drain. Fry the rest of the malpuas the same way. Fried malpuas taste best with tea.

If you prefer the malpuas dipped in syrup, then prepare the syrup by combining the sugar, water, cloves and cardamom in a heavy-bottomed saucepan. Place the pan over medium heat and bring it to a boil. Let it boil for 15 minutes. Turn off the heat. Add the fried malpuas to the hot syrup and turn them to coat. Let them soak for 15 minutes and then serve warm.

Rosh Boda

(Split Black Gram Fried Dumplings Soaked in Sugar Syrup)

Makes 25 dumplings

Deep-fried split black gram fritters are dipped in sugar syrup, which then turns them into spongy sweet dumplings. The tricky part of this dessert is making the fritters airy. A little bit of muscle work is required in aerating the batter before frying. You could also use a stand mixer and whisk the batter for a while to incorporate air into it. It is this airy, puffy texture that makes *rosh boda* such a light dessert, even though it's deep-fried.

Key Notes: Whisking the batter is very important for the airy texture of the dumplings. You could use a hand whisk, a stand mixer or a blender. Also, do not let the batter rest once you whisk it.

1 cup (200 g) split black gram

¼ tsp salt

2 cups (473 ml) water

2 cups (383 g) sugar

6 green cardamom pods

Oil, for deep-frying

In a bowl, soak the split black gram in water to cover for 4 hours. After 4 hours, the split black gram will puff up and soften a bit. Using a colander, drain the split black gram, transfer to a blender along with the salt and blend until you have a smooth batter. It shouldn't feel grainy at all. Add 2 tablespoons (30 ml) of water if needed. The batter shouldn't be runny and should be thick enough to hold its shape when added to the hot oil.

Transfer the batter to a bowl (or keep in the blender) and whisk for 5 minutes. This step is very important, as it will make the fritters airy and light.

To prepare the sugar syrup, add the water and sugar to a 9-inch (23-cm), heavy-bottomed saucepan and place it over medium-high heat. Add the green cardamom and bring it to a boil. Then let it simmer over medium heat for 15 minutes.

In the meantime, place another saucepan over medium heat and pour in the oil to reach a depth of 2 inches (5 cm). Also layer a plate with a kitchen towel.

Once the oil reaches 300°F (149°C), take a small cookie scooper and carefully scoop the batter into the hot oil. Do not overcrowd the pan. Fry for 7 to 10 minutes, turning the fritters every now and then to make sure they turn evenly golden. Using a slotted spoon, transfer the fritters to the kitchen towel.

The syrup should be ready after 15 minutes of simmering. Turn off the heat. Add the fried fritters to the hot syrup. Using a spoon, toss the fritters in the hot syrup every now and then. Leave the fritters in the syrup for about 30 minutes before serving.

Khejur Gur Er Mishti Doi

(Date Molasses Thick Yogurt)

Serves 4

Bengalis have a huge sweet tooth and most days, a meal ends with something sweet. One of the common everyday desserts is *mishti doi* from a nearby sweet shop. It's thick and creamy with the perfect amount of sweetness from caramelized sugar. It is made in an earthenware pot, which also enhances the flavor. I like to prepare mishti doi with *khejur gur* (date molasses). It not only gives that aromatic date flavor but also the rich amber shade.

Key Notes: If you cannot find jaggery, date molasses or caramelized sugar can be used instead. It's very important not to move the container as the yogurt sets overnight in a warm oven.

1⅔ cups (408 g) plain Greek yogurt

½ cup (118 ml) condensed milk

½ cup (118 ml) heavy cream

½ cup (72 g) grated jaggery

Place a cheesecloth or muslin cloth in a colander and place the colander in a large pot. Pour the Greek yogurt into the cheesecloth, bring the corners together and squeeze out as much water as you can. Then tie the corners of the cheesecloth and place it back in the colander. Set aside for an hour to allow any remaining water to drain off. This will turn into hung yogurt once the water is completely drained off.

Combine the condensed milk and heavy cream in a heavy-bottomed saucepan and place it over medium heat. Allow the milk to warm up, stirring continuously. Then add the grated jaggery and continue whisking for a minute or until the jaggery has completely dissolved and mixed with the milk. Remove from the heat.

Preheat the oven to 350°F (177°C).

Untie the cheesecloth and add the hung yogurt to the cream and jaggery mixture. Whisk for 2 minutes or until it forms a smooth, creamy consistency.

Pour the mixture into an ovenproof vessel, preferably an earthenware vessel. Cover it with aluminum foil and place it on the middle rack of the oven. Bake for 5 minutes. Then turn off the oven, turn on the oven light and allow it to rest inside the oven for 8 hours. Do not shake or move the container, as that will disturb the whole process of setting the yogurt.

After 8 hours, remove the container from the oven and place it in the refrigerator for 4 more hours. Mishti doi tastes best when served cold.

Kheer Er Sondesh

(Solid Milk Fudge)

Makes 15 pieces

Kheer er sondesh always takes me back to my childhood days. Ma has a huge, heavy brass wok, which she has always used to prepare solid milk (*kheer*). She would slow simmer gallons of milk for hours, turning it into a thick solid milk dough. While the dough is still warm, she presses small amounts into molds and creates sweet fudge. We never had cookie jars growing up, but kheer er sondesh was always there. These days, solid milk is sold in most Indian stores in the frozen section, thereby making it so easy for us to create as much sondesh as we want without breaking a sweat.

Key Notes: It's important to prepare the fudge while the dough is still warm because it hardens as it starts to cool down. I use a traditional sondesh mold, but you could also use candy molds or just roll out the dough and use a cookie cutter to make shapes. When you prepare the sondesh, it will be very fragile, but once you let it set, it hardens and stores for days in airtight jars.

12 oz (341 g) solid milk

3 tbsp (36 g) sugar

½ cup (118 ml) milk

1 tbsp (14 g) ghee

Using a grater, grate the solid milk into a nonstick pan. Place the pan over low heat. Add the sugar and milk. Stir.

As the pan heats up, the solid milk will start to soften, turning the entire mixture into a loose roux. Keep stirring constantly for 15 minutes until the mixture turns into a tighter dough.

After 15 minutes, turn off the heat and transfer the mixture to a bowl.

You need to shape the sondesh while the dough is still warm. If you have molds, then rub some ghee on the molds and press 1 tablespoon (11 g) of the dough into each mold. Press it evenly, about 1 millimeter thick, and press the edges to give a smooth, finished appearance. Carefully remove the pressed dough from the mold and place it on a plate. It will still be quite fragile, so handle carefully. Repeat with the remaining dough. The sondesh sets as it rests and cools, about an hour at room temperature.

Chitoi Pitha

(Steamed Rice Pancakes)

Serves 4

This is a long-lost recipe that people barely prepare these days. It's a steamed pancake prepared with just rice flour, without any oil or butter in it. Ma prepares it every time I visit home and I love it for breakfast. With freshly grated coconut and a little bit of shaved jaggery, it makes for a very healthy dish. Some days, I like to make it extra special by drizzling some creamy jaggery sauce on top.

Key Notes: Preparing these pancakes can be a little tricky. Make sure you use a nonstick pan. Also, you need a lid that will sit in the pan and not on the edge, so pick a lid that is smaller than the pan but big enough to cover the pancakes. You want space to sprinkle water around the edge of the lid to create the steam that cooks the pancakes. While preparing the pancakes, if you see that the bubbles are not forming or the batter is spreading too much, then add a bit more whole wheat flour to adjust the consistency.

FOR THE PANCAKES

1 cup (151 g) rice flour

¼ cup (25 g) whole wheat flour

Pinch of salt

1¼ cups (296 ml) water, or as needed

FOR THE JAGGERY CREAM SAUCE

¼ cup (36 g) grated jaggery, plus more for garnish

1 cup (237 ml) heavy cream

Freshly grated coconut, for garnish

To make the pancakes, whisk together the rice flour, whole wheat flour and salt in a mixing bowl. Pour in water little by little and whisk to make the batter. The consistency of the batter should be like pancakes or dosa batter—not too runny and not too thick. Allow the batter to rest for about 10 minutes.

To make the sauce, add the grated jaggery to a deep, heavy-bottomed saucepan over medium heat. Allow it to simmer until the jaggery starts melting. Now, very carefully, taking your face away from the pan, add the cream and give it a stir. Continue simmering for 5 minutes or until the sauce thickens and coats the back of a spoon.

To steam the pancakes, place a nonstick pan over medium heat and when the pan heats up, ladle a little bit of the batter into the center. Immediately cover with a lid that fits over the pancake and sits in the pan. Sprinkle 1 tablespoon (15 ml) of water all around the lid. It will start steaming the pancake, and in 2 to 3 minutes, you will see tiny bubbles appearing on top. Remove the lid and, using a spatula, carefully transfer the pancake to a plate. Repeat to use up the remaining batter.

Serve the warm *pithas* with the jaggery sauce, garnished with grated coconut and grated jaggery.

Snack and Sip

Snacking and sipping (*jol khabbar*) happen throughout the day. Bengalis are *khado roshisk* (food enthusiasts) and, therefore, snack time isn't necessarily restricted to just evening teatime. With all the courses that are traditionally prepared for lunch, lunchtime obviously gets delayed most days. So, the craving for a midmorning snack is pretty normal. A cup of *aada tejpata chaa* (ginger bay leaf milk tea) with something light to munch on, or *doi ghol* (sweet yogurt and jaggery smoothie) on brutal summer days, is a custom that most families follow.

Kolkata city is packed with friendly street food vendors, always tempting us to take a bite. They serve a wide variety of snacks and sips throughout the day. There are a few favorites that I feast on every time we visit Kolkata, and I share those with you in this section.

The sip section has yogurt smoothies, both sweet and spicy versions. The smoky green mango lemonade is a must for every summer. Then there is a fizzy drink that I absolutely love to make whenever my pantry becomes loaded with mint and ginger.

Kolkata Eggroll

(Crispy Layered Flatbread Wrapped with Egg)

Makes 5

One of my all-time favorite street foods from the city is the Kolkata eggroll. The crispy-layered *paratha* (flatbread) is wrapped in a thin layer of omelet, filled with a simple salad of crispy cucumber and onion and given a good squeeze of ketchup on top.

FOR THE LAYERED PARATHA

1½ cups (187 g) all-purpose flour

½ cup (50 g) whole wheat flour

1 tsp salt

1 tsp sugar

1½ tbsp (22 g) ghee

¾ cup (177 ml) warm water

7 tsp (35 ml) oil, divided

FOR THE FILLING

1 cup (151 g) finely sliced red onion

Lime wedges

1 cup (161 g) finely sliced cucumber

1 Indian green chilli, finely chopped (optional)

Ketchup

FOR THE OMELET

5 eggs

1 tsp salt

½ tsp freshly cracked black pepper

2½ tsp (12 ml) oil, divided

To make the layered paratha, in a mixing bowl, combine the flours, salt, sugar and ghee. Mix with your hands until it feels like crumbs. Then make a well in the center and pour in the warm water. Knead for 5 minutes or until the dough feels smooth and soft. Once done, rub a little oil on the dough and place it back in the mixing bowl. Cover with plastic wrap and let it rest for 20 minutes.

To make the filling, place the sliced red onion in a bowl and sprinkle with fresh lime juice. Stir and set aside. After 20 minutes, divide the dough into 5 equal portions. Roll each portion into a ball and cover it with a kitchen towel to keep the dough from getting dried out. Take one ball and rub some flour on it, and then roll the ball into a thin disk. Rub some oil on top and then, starting from one edge, fold the disk, like pleats. Each fold should be the width of your finger. Press every time you make a fold. Once done, hold the pleated log and then start folding firmly inward like a swirl. Pinch the end edge underneath the swirled disk. Cover with a kitchen towel and set aside. Continue shaping the rest of the dough.

Place a large pan, preferably cast-iron, over medium heat. As the pan heats up, take one of the swirled disks and roll it into a very thin disk. Add 1 teaspoon of the oil and carefully place the layered rolled disk on the hot pan. Using a spatula, press it all around to create a brown crust. Cook for about 2 minutes, then flip and cook for another 2 minutes, pressing it with a spatula. Transfer to a plate and cover. Repeat with more oil and the remaining disks of dough.

To make the omelet, crack the eggs into a mixing bowl. Add the salt and pepper and whisk until smooth. You can use the same pan that you used to prepare the paratha. Heat ½ teaspoon of the oil in the pan over medium-high heat and, when it's hot, add 3 tablespoons (44 ml) of the whisked egg. Swirl the pan to spread the egg, and then place one fried paratha on top. Press it down using the spatula. Cook on one side for a minute, then flip it over so the egg side is face up and transfer to a plate or chopping board. Continue cooking the remaining egg parathas.

To serve, layer the egg parathas with the egg side facing up. Layer on some onion followed by some cucumber and green chilli (if using) and then add some ketchup on top. Squeeze on some fresh lime juice. Wrap it tightly, using parchment paper or a paper towel, and serve immediately.

Ghugni

(Yellow Pea Stew)

Serves 4

In this recipe, dried yellow peas are soaked overnight and then slow-cooked with spices and potatoes into a comforting stew. Growing up, birthday party menus always included *ghugni* with *luchi* (page 17). On rainy days, ghugni would be served as an afterschool snack. It is also a very common street food in Kolkata.

Key Note: The yellow peas cook to a mushy consistency very quickly, so, keep an eye on the stew as you boil it because you want the peas to be tender but retain their shape.

1 cup (151 g) dried yellow peas

6 cups plus 1 tbsp (1.4 L) water, divided

2 tsp (10 g) salt, divided

½ tsp ground turmeric

1 tsp bhaja moshla (page 11)

½ tsp Indian chilli powder

1 tomato

1 medium potato

2 tbsp (30 ml) oil

1 tsp paanch phoron (page 11)

3 bay leaves

1 tsp sugar

½ tsp ground roasted fennel seeds

¼ cup (38 g) sliced red onion for garnish

¼ cup (12 g) finely chopped fresh cilantro for garnish

Lime wedges

Place the dried yellow peas in a bowl and add 2 cups (473 ml) of the water. Let them soak for 8 hours. After 8 hours, the peas will almost double in size and some peas will release the shell. Using a colander, drain the peas and then transfer to a heavy-bottomed saucepan. Add 3 cups (710 ml) of the water and 1 teaspoon of the salt and place the pan over high heat. Once the water comes to a boil, turn the heat down to medium, cover the pan with a lid and allow it to cook for 35 minutes or until the peas are tender. Drain the boiled peas in a colander and set aside.

In a small bowl, combine the turmeric, *bhaja moshla*, chilli powder and the 1 tablespoon (15 ml) of water. Stir and set aside.

Grate the tomato, peel the potato and cut it into big chunks and set both aside in separate bowls.

Place a heavy-bottomed pan over medium heat and add the oil. When the oil heats up, add the potato chunks and sprinkle with ½ teaspoon of salt. Let the potatoes fry for 5 minutes, tossing and turning every now and then. Remove from the pan and transfer to a bowl. Set aside.

To the same pan now add the *paanch phoron* and bay leaves and let sizzle for a few seconds, then pour in the reserved spice mixture. Stir and cook for 2 minutes. Add the grated tomato, the remaining ½ teaspoon of salt and the sugar and cook for 3 minutes, stirring occasionally. Add the boiled peas and mix everything together. Add the fried potatoes to the pan and toss to combine. Cook for 2 minutes, and then pour in the remaining 1 cup (237 ml) of water. Cover the pan and cook for 7 minutes.

Remove the lid, sprinkle the ground fennel seeds on top and cook for 2 more minutes. Check for salt and add any if required. If you prefer to have more gravy, add water and cook for a couple more minutes.

To serve, ladle the stew into bowls and garnish with some sliced red onion, fresh cilantro and a squeeze of fresh lime juice.

Jhaal Muri

(Spiced Puffed Rice)

Serves 2

Puffed rice is an essential part of Bengali cuisine. It is sometimes tossed in a hot pan with a little oil and nigella seeds until it turns crunchy. The crunchy and airy texture makes it a favorite snack, even for babies, after they start on their solid diet. *Jhaal muri*, literally translating to "spiced puffed rice," is a favorite street food in Kolkata. Every vendor has their own way of making it but the base pretty much remains the same: a quick toss of puffed rice with crunchy onion, cucumber, green chillies, some earthy spices and a good dose of mustard oil, served in an old newspaper.

Key Note: Jhaal muri should be served and relished as soon as it is prepared. If you allow it to rest, the puffed rice will turn soggy.

1 tbsp (8 g) cumin seeds

1 tsp fennel seeds

¼ cup (40 g) peanuts

1 tsp Indian chilli powder

1 tsp dried mango powder

1 tsp salt

4 tbsp (59 ml) mustard oil

3 cups (64 g) puffed rice

¼ cup (38 g) finely chopped red onion

¼ cup (40 g) finely chopped cucumber

¼ cup (50 g) peeled, boiled and diced potatoes

1 Indian green chilli, finely chopped

¼ cup (12 g) finely chopped cilantro

¼ cup (29 g) Bengal gram vermicelli

Place a small pan over medium-high heat and when the pan heats up, dry roast the cumin and fennel seeds for a few seconds. Transfer to a spice grinder or mortar and pestle and grind to a fine powder.

In the same pan, dry roast the peanuts for a couple of minutes. Transfer to a bowl and set aside.

Place the fennel and cumin in a big mixing bowl. Add the chilli powder, dried mango powder, salt and mustard oil. Stir.

Add the puffed rice, red onion, cucumber, diced boiled potatoes, green chilli and roasted peanuts. Give a toss to mix everything. Taste for salt and add any if required.

Finally sprinkle with the finely chopped cilantro and Bengal gram vermicelli. Toss once again and serve immediately.

Chirer Pulao

(Mixed Vegetable Flattened Rice Pilaf)

Serves 2

Flattened rice is de-husked rice, which is then rolled into light, dry flakes. It's a very popular ingredient in India, used in breakfast and snacks. The rice, when soaked in water or milk, rehydrates and swells a little. Ma would make this pilaf quite often, typically as an afterschool snack or a weekend breakfast. She always loaded it with vegetables and kept it pure vegetarian with no onion or garlic.

Key Notes: Flattened rice comes in three varieties: thick, medium thin and very thin. For this kind of pilaf, the medium thin works best, as it doesn't require any soaking and the texture of the rice is retained instead of turning mushy.

1½ cups (217 g) medium-thin flattened rice

2 tbsp (30 ml) oil, divided

2 tbsp (19 g) peanuts

1 tsp black mustard seeds

2 Indian dried red chillies

5 oz (140 g) bite-size cauliflower florets

3.4 oz (97 g) bite-size diced potato

4 oz (116 g) bite-size chopped carrot

1 tsp salt

1 tbsp (12 g) sugar

½ tsp ground turmeric

4 oz (116 g) bite-size chopped green beans

¼ cup (38 g) frozen peas

Finely chopped fresh cilantro for garnish

2 lemon/lime wedges

Place the flattened rice in a colander and rinse under running water. Keep the flattened rice in the colander and set it aside to drain.

Place a skillet over medium heat and add ½ tablespoon (7 ml) of the oil. Once the oil heats up, add the peanuts and fry for a minute. Transfer the fried peanuts to a separate bowl.

To the same pan, add the remaining 1½ tablespoons (23 ml) of oil. Add the mustard seeds and dried red chilli. Let the spices sizzle for a few seconds, then add the cauliflower, potato and carrot. Sprinkle with the salt, sugar and turmeric. Cover the pan and cook for 7 minutes, tossing and turning, until the cauliflower and the potato are cooked through and tender.

Add the green beans and let cook for 3 minutes longer or until tender.

Finally, add the washed flattened rice and gently toss it around to mix with the vegetables. Add the frozen peas and the fried peanuts. Toss around and taste for salt and sugar. Add any if required. Cook for 2 minutes.

Add the finely chopped cilantro leaves and squeeze fresh lime/lemon juice on top. Serve warm.

Aam Pora Shorbot

(Roasted Green Mango Cooler)

Serves 4

Sometimes also referred to as *aam panna*, this is a popular summer sip. Charring the mango over an open fire adds a lovely smoky flavor to the drink. The process of charring is also said to diminish the heat in the mango, thereby making it more cooling and refreshing to the tummy.

Key Note: You can add other spices and herbs to create your own flavor combination.

2 large green mangoes

⅓ cup (64 g) brown or granulated sugar

½ tsp salt

1 tbsp (6 g) bhaja moshla (page 11)

4½ cups (1 L) cold water

Ice cubes

Score the mangoes all around and place over an open fire. Using tongs, turn them around every now and then until the mangoes feel soft to the touch, the skin turns a mild yellow color and the outside is charred. It should take 10 to 12 minutes.

Allow the mangoes to cool completely and then peel off and discard the skin.

Place the peeled mangoes in a mixing bowl and use your hands to squeeze and remove the pulp. Discard the pits.

Transfer the pulp to a blender and add the sugar, salt and *bhaja moshla*. Blend until smooth. Then add the cold water and blend once again. The texture should be smooth without any fiber.

Serve cold with some ice cubes.

Borhani

(Yogurt and Mint Spiced Cool Drink)

Serves 4

This is a must-have drink for wedding parties. After the heavy multi-course meal, you want something to cool your tummy. The balance of mint, cilantro, cumin and yogurt makes this drink the perfect digestive sip you want to end the meal with. It's a great thirst quencher on hot summer days too!

1 tsp cumin seeds

2 cups (490 g) thick Greek yogurt

1 cup (237 ml) water

⅓ cup (17 g) fresh mint leaves

⅓ cup (17 g) fresh cilantro leaves

1 Indian green chilli

1 tsp salt

2 tbsp (24 g) sugar

1 tsp freshly cracked black pepper

Lime wedges

Ice cubes

Place a small pan over medium-high heat and when it heats up, add the cumin seeds. Dry roast the cumin seeds for a few seconds, shaking the pan every now and then. Then using a mortar pestle or a grinder, grind it to a fine powder.

Transfer the cumin to a blender, add the rest of the ingredients except the lime juice and blend to a smooth consistency. Pour into a pitcher.

Squeeze some fresh lime juice into the pitcher and serve the drink with some ice cubes.

Aada Pudina Shorbot

(Ginger and Mint Fizz)

Serves 4

The combination of fresh mint and fresh ginger makes this drink one zesty thirst quencher. It also works as a great digestion aid after a heavy meal. I like to add sparkling water to the concentrated juice just before serving, but water would work well too.

1 tsp cumin seeds

1.2 oz (34 g) fresh ginger, peeled and chopped

½ cup (25 g) tightly packed fresh mint leaves, plus more for garnish

1 tsp salt

1 tsp sugar

3 tbsp (44 ml) freshly squeezed lemon juice

Ice cubes

2 cups (473 ml) sparkling water

Place a small pan over medium-high heat, let it heat up and then add the cumin seeds. Shake the pan for a few seconds and then turn off the heat.

In a blender, combine the ginger, mint leaves, salt, sugar, roasted cumin seeds and lemon juice. Blend until smooth and then strain it. At this stage, the juice will taste very strong and concentrated. It can be preserved in an airtight glass jar in the refrigerator for about a week.

When ready to serve, shake and pour some of the concentrated juice into a glass. Add some ice cubes, top with sparkling water and garnish with some fresh mint leaves.

Doi Ghol

(Yogurt and Jaggery Sweet Smoothie)

Serves 2

Yogurt drinks are prepared a lot during the summer and are the best way to cool down and beat the brutal Indian heat. There are several ways to flavor it up, sometimes savory and sometimes sweet. *Doi ghol* is mildly sweet and is flavored with jaggery. I love adding fresh ginger, as it gives a refreshing zing at the back of your palate.

1 cup (245 g) Greek yogurt

1 cup (237 ml) water

0.6 oz (20 g) fresh ginger, peeled and chopped

½ tsp salt

1.6 oz (50 g) jaggery

Ice cubes

Add everything except the ice to a blender and blend until smooth. Pour into a pitcher and serve with ice cubes.

Aada Tejpata Chaa

(Ginger Bay Leaf Milk Tea)

Makes 2 cups (473 ml)

Tea culture in India is a rhythm of daily life. Every other street corner has a tea stall, preparing and serving piping hot tea from the wee hours of the morning to late at night. It's a morning ritual for most of us that we find very hard to live without. You can prepare it with just tea leaves and milk or add spices to it; a cup of creamy Indian tea is soul satisfying. We like our morning tea with just ginger and bay leaves. The subtle heat from fresh ginger is absolutely uplifting.

Key Notes: It's very important to add the grated or pounded fresh ginger only after the milk heats up or else the milk might curdle. I like milk tea rich, so I always keep the ratio of milk to water 1:1.

1 cup (237 ml) water

1 cup (237 ml) whole milk

2½ tsp (10 g) sugar

1½ tsp (1 g) black tea leaves

1 bay leaf

1 tbsp (8 g) grated ginger

Combine the water, milk, sugar, tea leaves and bay leaf in a deep saucepan over high heat.

When the milk comes to a boil, turn down the heat to medium and add the fresh ginger. Stir and let it simmer for 2 minutes.

Turn off the heat and strain the ginger milk tea into two cups and serve immediately.

Playful Cooking

I grew up eating Bengali food and I like to stick to the authenticity of the dishes. But every once in a while, I like to add a twist. Arvind is not Bengali and we both love exploring different cuisines and trying out new flavors. This is the reason why my blog, Playful Cooking, isn't restricted to any specific kind of cuisine.

In this section, I took some of my favorite Bengali dishes and gave them a fun little twist. These dishes are easy to prepare nonetheless. It is just how I enjoy cooking—fuss free and quick.

A simple summer snack, *aam doi* (mango and yogurt) is prepared in the form of a tart, and everyone's favorite *patishapta* is served as a layered crepe cake. I added a playful touch to a few authentic dishes and I hope you enjoy the new approach to Bengali cuisine.

Fresh Cheese and White Chocolate Fudge

Makes 12

One of the famous Bengali desserts is *sondesh*, where fresh cheese (*chaana*) is sweetened and then shaped into sweet bites. I have shared a sondesh recipe on page 147 in my "Sweet Tooth" chapter. This fudge with fresh cheese and white chocolate is my take on good old sondesh. You get the sweetness of white chocolate, nutty almonds and fresh cheese, all blended together to form soft fudgy bites. It's easy to prepare, even for a big crowd.

9.3 oz (260 g) chaana (page 13)

5 oz (142 g) white chocolate, finely chopped

3 tbsp (18 g) almond flour

2 tbsp (19 g) raisins

2 tbsp (21 g) slivered almonds

Layer a loaf pan with parchment paper.

Place a heavy-bottomed pan over medium-low heat and add the chaana, finely chopped chocolate and almond flour. Stir and cook for 5 minutes, or until the mixture comes together and doesn't stick to the pan anymore.

Press the mixture firmly into the loaf pan to form a smooth surface. In a small bowl, combine the raisins and slivered almonds. Sprinkle the mixture on top and press lightly. Place the pan in the refrigerator for about 4 hours to set.

Turn out the fudge onto a cutting board and slice into 12 pieces. Serve or store in an airtight jar in the refrigerator.

Mango Yogurt Tart

Makes 4 tarts

The most exciting part of Indian summer is the abundance of mangoes in the market. One common way we enjoy ripe mangoes is by mixing it with yogurt. It's a great snack or a sweet treat at the end of a meal. I took the same concept and prepared these mini tarts. You get the same flavor of *aam doi* in the flaky texture of the crust.

FOR THE FILLING
1 cup (245 g) thick Greek yogurt
1 cup (246 g) mango puree

FOR THE CRUST
¾ cup (94 g) all-purpose flour
¼ cup (24 g) almond flour
½ cup (96 g) granulated sugar
4 tbsp (57 g) butter, softened
¼ tsp salt
1 tsp almond extract

FOR GARNISH
Sliced mango
Powdered sugar for dusting

To make the filling, layer a cheesecloth in a colander and spoon the Greek yogurt into the center of the cheesecloth. Gently bring up the corners and tie into a knot. Let the yogurt drain for 30 minutes.

In the meantime, prepare the crust. In a mixing bowl, combine both flours, granulated sugar, butter and salt. Using a fork or your hands, mix together into a crumb-like texture. Add the almond extract and give it one more mix. Add a little water if it feels too dry.

Divide the mixture among 4 mini tart pans and press it evenly into the bottom and up the sides. Use the back of a measuring spoon to press the crust into an even layer. Once done, place the mini tart pans in the refrigerator for 15 minutes.

Preheat the oven to 350°F (177°C).

Take the pans out of the fridge and, using a fork, poke the crust several times. Place the pans on a baking sheet and bake for 15 minutes or until lightly golden. Remove the pans from the oven and place on a cooling rack. Let the crust cool down slightly.

To finish the filling, scrape the yogurt off the cheesecloth into a mixing bowl. Add the mango puree and whisk to form a smooth consistency. Divide the mixture among the mini tart pans. Carefully cover the tops of the pans with aluminum foil.

If the oven is warm, place the prepared tart pans on a baking sheet. If the oven doesn't feel warm, preheat the oven, then turn it off and place the prepared tart in the oven for 8 hours.

Remove the pans from the oven and transfer to the refrigerator for 4 hours.

To garnish, layer the sliced mangoes on top, dust with powdered sugar and serve!

Mascarpone and Jaggery Filled Eggless Crepe Cake

Makes about 14 crepes

During the harvest festival, Bengalis prepare *pitha*. Pitha is not one type of sweet treat but a term used for desserts prepared using rice, jaggery (*patali gur*), coconut and flour. During this festival, Ma always prepares *patishapta*, a famous type of pitha. A runny batter of rice flour, semolina and all-purpose flour is used to prepare thin, crepe-like pancakes, which are then filled with either solid milk (*kheer*) or coconut mixed with jaggery. I took the same dish and gave it a little twist by styling it like a cake and filling it with a mix of mascarpone cheese and jaggery.

Key Notes: The batter needs to be runny to prepare thin crepes. Allow the crepes to cool before you start layering it with the whipped mascarpone cheese. If you can't find jaggery, you can replace it with brown sugar. Alternatively, you could serve the crepes individually with the filling.

1 cup (125 g) all-purpose flour

¼ cup (44 g) fine semolina

2 tbsp (19 g) rice flour

2 tbsp (24 g) granulated sugar

Pinch of salt

1 cup (237 ml) milk

½ cup (118 ml) water

2 tbsp (29 g) ghee

8 oz (227 g) mascarpone cheese

¼ cup (36 g) jaggery powder

Fresh fruits, such as berries, pitted cherries or sliced stone fruits

Powdered sugar, for dusting

In a mixing bowl, combine the flour, semolina, rice flour, granulated sugar and salt. Whisk to blend, and then pour in the milk and water. Whisk again to form a smooth batter. The batter should be runny. Add more milk if it's too thick or add more flour if it's too runny. Cover the bowl and let the batter rest for 30 minutes to 1 hour.

To prepare the crepes, place a nonstick pan over medium heat. Brush a little bit of ghee on the pan and pour ⅓ cup (60 g) of the batter mixture into the center of the pan. Quickly lift the pan off the stove and swirl it to spread the batter into a circular disk. You could also use the back of the spoon to spread the batter. Let it cook for 1 minute on one side, until you see bubbles appearing. Flip carefully as these are very fragile and can break easily, then cook for 1 more minute.

Transfer the cooked crepe to a plate. Continue cooking the rest of the crepes the same way.

Once all the crepes are ready, prepare the filling. Place the mascarpone cheese and jaggery in a mixing bowl and whisk to a smooth consistency.

To prepare the layered crepe cake, place one crepe on a serving plate. Spread with a little bit of the whipped mascarpone and top it with another crepe. Continue the process until all the crepes are layered and filled. Finally, spread the remaining whipped mascarpone cheese on top and garnish with fresh fruit. Dust with powdered sugar and serve.

Bottle Gourd Meringue Pudding

Serves 4

I grew up eating bottle gourd pudding a lot. It's called *lau payesh* or *lau dudh*. The pudding is light and takes less time to prepare than rice pudding. So, on busy weeknights, if Ma had to prepare a dessert, she would always make bottle gourd pudding. I took a different route with the pudding by keeping the consistency thick and then topped it with smoky charred meringue.

FOR THE PUDDING

1 lb (500 g) grated bottle gourd flesh (discard the seeds before grating)

1 tbsp (14 g) ghee

½ tsp ground cardamom

1 cup (237 ml) heavy cream

½ cup (121 g) cream cheese

¼ cup (48 g) sugar

FOR THE MERINGUE

3 egg whites

½ cup (96 g) sugar

To make the pudding, layer a cheesecloth in a colander and add the grated bottle gourd. Gather the corners of the cheesecloth into a knot and squeeze out as much water as you can. Then tie the corners and leave the cheesecloth in the colander for an hour to drain as much moisture as possible.

Place a heavy-bottomed pan over medium heat and add the ghee. Untie the cheesecloth and add the grated bottle gourd to the pan. Sprinkle with the cardamom and stir. Cook the bottle gourd for 5 minutes. The bottle gourd will soften and the raw flavor will be gone.

Pour in the heavy cream and stir. Cook for 5 minutes, and then add the cream cheese and sugar. Cook for a couple more minutes or until the pudding thickens. Check for sugar and add any if required.

Turn off the heat and scrape the pudding into 2 serving bowls. You could also just use one big serving bowl or divide among 4 individual small bowls. (If you will be placing the bowls under the broiler instead of using a kitchen torch, make sure you use ovenproof vessels.) Cover the bowls with plastic wrap and place in the refrigerator for an hour to set. You can also make the pudding a couple of days in advance and keep refrigerated.

When ready to serve, make the meringue. Place the egg whites in a clean, dry mixing bowl. Use an electric mixer to whisk the egg whites to stiff peaks. Then add the sugar, little by little and continue whisking until the meringue looks glossy white and stays stiff when the whisk is lifted up. Layer the meringue on top of the pudding and use the back of a spoon to form swirls.

To create the smoky char, either use a kitchen torch or place the bowls on the top rack of the oven under the broiler for a few seconds. Keep an eye if you are placing it under the broiler, because it chars very quickly.

Serve immediately. If you used 2 bowls, divide each in half to serve 4.

Quinoa Split Yellow Beans Pilaf

Serves 2

If you enjoy *bhoger khichuri* (split mung beans and rice porridge, page 22), then you will enjoy this pilaf a lot. It has a similar flavor except that instead of using rice, I used quinoa. It's equally hearty and comforting with hard-boiled eggs, the pop of fresh mint leaves and extra crunch from pomegranate seeds.

½ cup (100 g) split yellow mung beans

¾ cup (94 g) white quinoa

4 cups (946 ml) water

1 tsp salt

½ tsp ground turmeric

3 tbsp (43 g) ghee

1 tsp paanch phoron (page 11)

½ onion, thinly sliced

2 tbsp (30 ml) fresh lime juice

¼ cup (12 g) fresh mint leaves

¼ cup (38 g) pomegranate seeds

2 hard-boiled eggs, cut in half (optional)

Using a colander, wash the split yellow mung beans several times under running water and add to a bowl. Add water to cover and let the beans soak for 15 minutes. After 15 minutes, drain the beans and return them to the bowl.

Simultaneously, soak the quinoa in a bowl of water for 5 minutes. This helps remove the bitter taste. After 5 minutes, pour the soaked quinoa into a colander and wash it several times under running water.

Place a deep, heavy-bottomed saucepan over high heat and add the 4 cups (946 ml) of water. Add the split yellow beans, quinoa, salt and turmeric and bring the water to a boil. Once it comes to a boil, reduce the heat to medium and let it simmer for 25 minutes or until the beans are cooked through. Remove from the heat.

Heat the ghee in a separate small skillet over medium heat. Add the *paanch phoron* and cook for a few seconds, and then add the sliced onion. Cook the onion for about 5 minutes or until it softens. Scrape the contents of the pan on top of the cooked yellow beans and quinoa. Add the fresh lime juice and stir to combine. Ladle the porridge into a serving bowl and garnish with the mint leaves, pomegranate seeds and hard-boiled eggs, if using. Serve warm.

Red Lentil Falafel

Makes 15 falafel

I took the humble *daaler boda* (red lentil fritters, page 38) and gave it the Middle Eastern falafel approach. The spice combination works beautifully with the aroma of red lentils. It's crunchy on the outside and soft inside, which makes it perfect to serve with some chilled drinks on the side. I enjoy it with a dollop of tahini sauce on top, but you can always serve it with just ketchup or any other dipping sauce of your choice.

½ cup (100 g) split red lentils

1 tsp coriander seeds

½ tsp cumin seeds

½ tsp fennel seeds

½ cup (76 g) finely chopped red onion

1 Indian green chilli

¼ cup (12 g) fresh cilantro leaves

1 tsp white sesame seeds

1 tbsp (5 g) desiccated coconut

½ tsp freshly cracked black pepper

1 tsp salt

Oil, for deep-frying

Tahini sauce, for serving (optional)

Place the lentils in a deep bowl and pour in 1 cup (237 ml) of water. Let soak for 3 hours.

Place a small pan over medium-high heat, and when the pan heats up, add the coriander seeds, cumin seeds and fennel seeds. Dry roast for about a minute by tossing the pan frequently to avoid burning. Once done, place the roasted seeds on a plate and allow to cool down a bit. Then coarsely grind the seeds in a spice grinder or mortar and pestle.

After 3 hours, when the lentils have puffed up, drain off any excess water and place the lentils in a food processor with the chopping blade attached. Run the food processor and grind the lentils to a coarse consistency. Do not let it turn into a paste or you will not get the crunch in the falafel. Transfer to a mixing bowl.

To the food processor now add the onion, green chilli and cilantro leaves. Run the food processor to finely chop everything. Transfer to the same bowl with the lentils.

Now to the bowl, add the spice powder, sesame seeds, desiccated coconut, black pepper and salt and stir to combine.

Take 1 heaping tablespoon (10 g) of the mixture and, using your hands, shape into a tiny ball. Shape the rest of the mixture the same way. You should get about 15 falafel.

Place a heavy-bottomed saucepan over medium heat and add the oil to reach a depth of 2 inches (5 cm). Layer a plate with a kitchen towel. Once the oil reaches 350°F (177°C), very carefully add the shaped balls, without overcrowding the pan. Fry for about 5 minutes, tossing and turning, until golden brown in color. Using a slotted spoon, transfer the falafel to the kitchen towel to drain the excess oil.

Serve hot, drizzling some tahini sauce on top if desired.

Spiced Salmon in Swiss Chard

Serves 4

Ma makes a dish where dried fish is cooked with spices, wrapped in pumpkin leaves and then coated with a light batter before deep-frying to a crispy texture. The dish is prepared with a certain kind of dried fish that is not available in the United States. I took the same concept and gave it a modern twist by using salmon and wrapping it with Swiss chard leaves.

1 small red onion

3 tbsp (45 ml) oil, divided

1 tsp grated ginger

1 tbsp (10 g) grated garlic

1 tsp salt, divided

1 tsp turmeric, divided

½ tsp sugar

½ tsp ground cumin

½ tsp ground coriander

1 tsp Indian chilli powder

4 Swiss chard leaves

4 salmon fillets (approximately 2 oz/ 54 g each)

1 tbsp (8 g) all-purpose flour

1 tbsp (10 g) rice flour

1½ tablespoons (22 ml) water

Finely chop the onion. Place a heavy-bottomed pan over medium heat and add 1 tablespoon (15 ml) of the oil. When the oil heats up, add the onion, ginger and garlic. Sprinkle with ½ teaspoon of the salt, ½ teaspoon of the turmeric and the sugar. Stir and cook for 3 minutes.

Sprinkle with the cumin, coriander and chilli powder. Stir and cook for about 7 minutes or until the raw smell of the onion is gone and the spices are cooked through. You should see the oil being released from the sides. Turn off the heat and let it cool to room temperature.

In the meantime, clean the Swiss chard leaves and trim off the hard stem. Depending on how big the leaves are and how hard the stems are, you can trim off a little bit from the edge of the leaf too.

Fill a 9-inch (23-cm) pan with water and place over medium heat. When the water comes to a boil, turn off the heat. Dip the leaves, without overcrowding the pan, and allow them to soften for about 3 minutes. Then very carefully take the leaves out of the hot water and place on a chopping board.

Working with one leaf at a time, place 1 tablespoon (13 g) of the cooled onion spice mixture on the lower edge of the leaf. Then place one salmon fillet on top of it and place another tablespoon (13 g) of the mixture on top of the salmon. Wrap the fish carefully by rolling the leaf upward. Fold both sides of the leaf into the center, press it slightly and then keep rolling upward. Set aside, folded side down, and wrap the rest of the salmon the same way.

In a small bowl, combine the all-purpose flour, rice flour, remaining ½ teaspoon of salt and remaining ½ teaspoon of turmeric. Add the water and stir to make a batter.

To shallow fry the wrapped fish, place a pan over medium heat and add the remaining 2 tablespoons (30 ml) of oil. Layer a plate with a kitchen towel. When the oil heats up, very gently roll one wrapped fish in the batter. Carefully place it in the hot pan. Fry for 2 minutes on each side and then transfer to the kitchen towel to drain any excess oil. Fry the rest of the wrapped fish the same way.

Serve immediately, as it tastes best when hot.

Essential Ingredients Used in Bengali Cooking

Spices

A lot of whole spices are used in everyday cooking, and these whole spices bring out the aroma of the dish. Unlike in Western cuisines, whole spices like cinnamon sticks, bay leaves or cardamom pods are not removed before serving a meal. It is left to the diner to pick them out and set them aside. Having said this, there is no harm in removing any whole spices just before serving, except for dishes like biryani, where it might be difficult to pick them out before serving.

Nigella Seeds (*Kalo Jeere*) These tiny black seeds with a rounded triangle shape are used in several dishes. Nigella is always used whole and this mild, peppery spice has a pungent taste. Ma also uses nigella seeds in a very unique way to enhance her appetite when she falls ill and the medicines ruin her taste buds. She dry roasts the seeds and then grinds them to a fine powder. Then, she mixes it with hot steamed rice with a sprinkle of salt and ghee (clarified butter). The pungent taste of the spice also works as a palate cleanser.

Cumin Seeds (*Jeere*) Cumin is one of the most commonly used spices in Bengali cooking. The warm and earthy aroma of this slightly curved, ridged, pale brown whole spice makes it extremely versatile. When dry roasted and crushed, the shade turns to deep brown and the flavor gets very strong.

Black Mustard Seeds (*Kalo Shorshe*) These tiny black seeds are yet another very common spice. It's always used at the beginning of cooking by adding it to the hot oil, which makes it pop and release an aromatic, nutty flavor. It's more pungent than yellow mustard seeds and a tiny amount goes a long way. It's mostly used as a whole spice except when you are making *kashundi* (mango mustard sauce).

Yellow Mustard Seeds (*Shada Shorshe*) These yellow seeds are used a lot in Bengali cuisine in the form of a paste. The seed on its own doesn't have any aroma and the whole seed is rarely used in cooking. But when ground with green chillies, it is called *shorshe baata* (page 11). This creamy, pungent paste is used in several dishes, be it fish, chicken, egg or vegetable. It is a favorite for our palate.

Fennel Seeds (*Mouri*) This slightly curved, oval-shaped spice with a sweet anise flavor is used a lot in Bengali cuisine. It is sometimes used whole and sometimes roasted and then ground into a fine powder. The color ranges from dark green to mild yellow; pick the dark green shade for the best flavor. Apart from being a very common mouth freshener, fennel is one of those spices that is used in both sweet and savory dishes.

Fenugreek Seeds (*Methi*) This bright yellow, roughly octagonal-shaped seed has a pungent and bitter flavor. Just like black mustard seeds, this spice is also added to hot oil at the beginning of cooking. In Bengali cuisine, it's not used a lot directly except for *paanch phoron* (Bengali five spice).

Bengali Five-Spice Powder (*Paanch Phoron [page 11]*) One of the most commonly used spice mixes in Bengali dishes is paanch phoron, also known as Indian five spice mix. Paanch means "five" and phoron means "tempering," because it's used for tempering and goes very well with lentil stew, vegetable stir-fries, pickles and any rich fish and meat curries.

Coriander Seeds (*Dhone*) This spherical, ribbed, pale brown seed makes its appearance in several cuisines. In Bengali dishes, this particular spice is rarely used whole. It's roasted and powdered along with a couple of other spices to make a very common Bengali spice mix called *bhaja moshla*.

Bhaja Moshla (page 11) This spice mix is unique to Bengali cuisine. It's almost as essential as *gorom moshla* except that it is not necessarily used only in cooking. It's often used right at the end of cooking for a flavor boost, and sometimes even as garnish. Every household makes their own version of bhaja moshla, and my version in this book is the one that I learned to make from Ma. You should never make spice mixes in large batches because the flavor dies over a period of time. I always prefer making this in small batches.

Clove (*Lobongo*) This spice is highly aromatic, warm and mildly peppery. It is used whole at the beginning of cooking in hot oil, mostly for rich dishes. It's also used to enhance the flavor of sugar syrup for desserts.

Green Cardamom (*Elach*) The delicate, citrusy, sweet fragrance and warmth of green cardamoms make it one of the most popular spices in India. It is used in rich curries and in desserts. At the beginning of cooking, it is used whole in hot oil and the seeds are crushed into a fine powder for desserts. Just like clove, green cardamom is also used to enhance the essence of sugar syrup for desserts.

Cinnamon (*Daar Chini*) Cinnamon sticks are warm and sweet. Just like clove and cardamom, the spice is versatile and can be used in both sweet and savory dishes. It can be used as a whole stick or ground into a powder.

Bengali *Gorom Moshla* (page 11) There are different versions of this roasted, flavorful spice mix. The Bengali version is flavorful but not spicy. It is added at the end of cooking to mainly enhance the flavor. As with all spice mixes, make small batches to preserve the flavor.

White Poppy Seeds (*Posto*) Nutty, fragrant white poppy seeds are extremely common in Bengali dishes. It is often used in the form of a creamy paste. This spice goes really well with vegetarian dishes. I have some friends who are so fond of posto that they use it in some form or another in their daily meals.

Sesame Seeds (*Till*) This teardrop-shaped flat seed might not have a lot of aroma but the nutty sweet flavor makes it a great addition to chutney and sweet treats. Whether you are using black or white sesame seeds, dry roasting always enhances the flavor.

Turmeric (*Holud*) This is one of the key spices used in Indian cuisine. Turmeric is a digestive and an antiseptic, has a mild earthy flavor and gives the vibrant yellow shade to most Indian dishes. Typically, ground turmeric is used in cooking and raw turmeric is used to make healthy drinks. You have to be careful while using turmeric because it can stain easily.

Chillies

Indian Green Chillies (*Lonka*) Most Bengali dishes are not fiery spicy. The flavor is mellow and the heat is mostly from fresh green chillies. Sometimes green chillies are finely chopped and sometimes they are split in half. There are different kinds of chillies grown in India and the most commonly used green chillies are *jwala* and *dhani*.

Indian Dried Red Chillies (*Shukna Lonka*) Dried red chillies are extremely common for adding depth of flavor to Indian cooking. They are often added at the beginning of cooking in hot oil to infuse the flavor. There are different varieties of red chillies used in India. Grinding dried red chillies into powder enhances the flavor and the heat level. Chilli powder is used rarely in Bengali cooking. However, the Kashmiri chilli is one kind of dried red chilli that is mostly used to add a vibrant red shade without adding heat to a dish.

Herbs

Bay Leaves (*Tej Paata*) The flavor of fresh bay leaves is strong and can taste bitter. Therefore, dried bay leaves are often used in cooking. It is one of the most commonly used herbs in Bengali cooking. Apart from using it in savory dishes at the beginning of cooking, Ma uses bay leaves in sweet puddings to infuse the milk and in milk tea.

Cilantro Leaves (*Dhone Paata*) Also referred to as coriander leaves, this is one of the most commonly used herbs in Indian cooking. Just a little amount of finely chopped cilantro leaves adds the vibrant color pop that most Indian curries need. Both the leaves and the stem are used in preparing chutneys and they are often added in fritters.

Mint Leaves (*Pudina Paata*) Of the different varieties of mint leaves that are available, the dark green spearmint is most common in India. It is often used to prepare chutney. In Bengali cooking, it is not that often used, unless you are making cool drinks like *aada pudina shorbot* (page 163) and *borhani* (page 161).

Oils and Fats

Mustard Oil (*Shorshe Tel*) Mustard oil to Bengalis is what olive oil is to Italians. It's used in cooking and even consumed raw by mixing into certain dishes and sauces. The oil has a very distinctive, pungent flavor and it is an acquired taste. You sniff the oil and it will hit your sinuses. Mustard oil has a long list of medicinal properties and is becoming more common across the globe. The high smoke point makes it good for deep-frying. It is definitely high in calories, which is why the use of this oil these days is restricted to a few dishes only to enhance the flavor.

Clarified Butter (Ghee) When you slow simmer unsalted butter, it cooks out all the impurities, giving you a smooth golden, clarified butter. It is the most refined end product of milk and it plays a significant role in every Indian household. Savory or sweet, festive season or regular meal, ghee happens to makes an appearance quite often. Although Bengalis don't always cook with ghee, in most vegetarian dishes a tiny dollop is added at the end of cooking for a nutty flavor boost.

Rice and Lentils

Gobindo Bhog This short-grain, aromatic rice is cultivated in West Bengal. The flavor is sweet and buttery. A lot of rice dishes, sweet and savory, are prepared with gobindo bhog rice.

Split Bengal Gram (*Chana Daal*) This is mildly sweet and has a firm texture. The texture of this lentil is hard and needs a few hours of soaking before you start cooking with it. Famous Bengali *cholar daal* (page 63) is prepared using this lentil.

Red Split Lentil (*Mushuri Daal*) This is one of the most common lentils used in any Indian kitchen. *Daal* (lentil stew) is a must at every meal and most often, it's the red split lentil that is used because it cooks faster than any other variety.

Yellow Split Mung Bean (*Mung Daal*) This is one of those beans that can be eaten raw as well as cooked. The beans are petite and have an olive-green skin. When soaked for several hours, the bean softens, making it perfect for salads and snacks. The other two varieties of this bean are split with skin and without skin. Both of them are used to prepare stew and porridge. In Bengali cooking, the split bean without the skin is used quite often to prepare lentil stew and porridge. Often, the beans are first roasted dry to give them a nutty aroma. This bean is also used to prepare sweet dishes.

Yellow Peas (*Motor*) These dried peas look white, but when soaked in water they puff up in size and change to a mild yellow shade. These peas are used to make thick stew called *ghugni* (page 154), a very famous street food in Kolkata.

Split Skinless Black Lentils (*Biuli Daal*) This protein-rich, energy booster lentil is prepared in several ways. When it's whole with the skin on, it's used to prepare thick, rich lentil stew, which is very famous in the region of Punjab. When the skin is removed and it's split, the flavor is subtler, making it perfect for a light lentil stew, savory crispy fritters or light, airy desserts such as *rosh boda* (page 143).

Sweet and Sour

Jaggery (*Gur*) Jaggery is a natural sweetener prepared from concentrated sugarcane juice or date or palm sap, creating various flavors. Depending on the source of extraction, the color of jaggery can vary from light brown to dark brown. A common kind of jaggery used in Bengali cooking is *khejur gur/patali gur* (page 25). It is derived from the sap of the date palm tree and is a rich burgundy color. The flavor is sweet and aromatic, which makes it a perfect natural sweetener for desserts. This particular type of jaggery is not readily available outside of Bengali stores; a good substitute is date molasses.

Tamarind (*Tetul*) Tamarind fruits are thick and curved, and range from 1½ to 4¾ inches (4 to 12 cm) long. Inside the pod, you will find a sticky fibrous brown pulp and inside the pulp are the brown seeds. The seeds are removed, and the pulp is boiled and turned into a paste. This paste is used to add acidity to different dishes and chutneys. Of course, these days it is easy to find the readymade concentrated tamarind paste in any supermarket.

Green Mango (*Kacha Aam*) Green mango is consumed a lot in Bengali culture. It's used in different ways to add a smack to the palate. From raw mango mash kache (*aam makha*, page 119) and chutney (*kacha aamer*, page 123) to sauces (*kashundi*, page 116) and drinks (*aam pora shorbot*, page 163), it is a favorite souring agent that is used in a lot of dishes.

Flours

Wheat Flour (*Atta*) One of the most common flours used in preparing Indian flatbread, atta is milled from durum wheat, a variety of hard wheat. The dough comes out soft and is easy to roll out thin. *Ruti* (page 14) is prepared with wheat flour and is often eaten at breakfast or dinner with several sides.

All-Purpose Flour (*Moida*) Similar to cake flour, all-purpose flour is refined and finely milled without any bran. This white flour is commonly used in Bengali cuisine to prepare *luchi* (page 17), unlike in the rest of India, where atta is typically used to prepare this fried mini flatbread.

Rice Flour (*Chaaler Gudo*) The finely milled, gluten-free flour from rice is used a lot in Bengali cooking, especially to prepare desserts. I always like to add rice flour to the batter for deep-fried dishes because it adds a nice crispiness to it.

Chickpea Flour (Beshon) Also known as gram flour, this flour is made from a variety of pulses and quite commonly used to make the batter for anything deep-fried. The flour is also used widely to prepare desserts and various curries.

Fish

Fish is the most dominant protein used in everyday Bengali meals. There are several selections of freshwater fishes available, which give us a wide variety of choice. Unlike other parts of India, Bengalis eat every part of the fish, except of course the fins and innards. The fish head is a delicacy for us and there are various ways to prepare it (pages 32 and 66).

Of the forty or so varieties of freshwater fish available, I have used the following four and have mentioned a substitute for each in the recipe section.

Rohu Fish (*Rui Mach*) This large, silver-colored fish can reach up to a length of 6 feet (1.8 m). It belongs to the carp family of fish and is the most commonly used fish for everyday cooking.

Hilsa Fish (*Ilish Mach*) This freshwater fish belongs to the herring family of fish. It's an oily fish and rich in omega-3 fatty acids. In Bengali cooking, this fish has great importance and is used in gourmet dishes. It's mostly available during winter season. It is not only customary but also considered auspicious to prepare Ilish on special occasions.

Pabo Catfish (*Papda Mach*) The soft flesh, smooth skin and just one center bone makes this one of the easiest to eat Bengali fish. It's fast to cook and takes on flavors well. The taste is also very delicate, which makes it a favorite for children to enjoy. Because of the tender flesh, frying this fish is tricky as it can splatter a lot. So, be very careful and make sure you have a tight-fitting lid for the pan before you fry the fish.

Tangra Mach This is a small, freshwater fish of the catfish family. The fish has soft flesh and a mild flavor, which makes it quite versatile to use in many different ways, from crispy fried to a mild tangy broth. Tangra maach is one of the most common small fish used in everyday Bengali cooking.

Acknowledgments

A project like this can never happen singlehandedly. I cannot thank all my friends and family enough for helping me make this dream come true.

Both my husband and I are lucky to have no dietary restrictions. It allows us to indulge in different kinds of cuisines and flavors. It also gives me the freedom to cook different kinds of dishes every day. But during the entire process of writing this cookbook, I mostly prepared Bengali meals, even repeating the same dish multiple times in a week. Arvind didn't complain one bit. Instead, he only helped me get better. His constant support is something I can never explain in words. He has made a major contribution to what I am today and I can never thank him enough!

My Ma is an amazing cook and always has been. My entire family, including all my aunts and uncles, my cousins and my friends, absolutely relish everything she prepares. She is not a gourmet cook and prepares only Bengali food, things she learned from my Grandma. Throughout the journey of writing this book, Ma spent several hours on the phone with me, giving me the recipe ideas and sharing stories. Because she never cooks using measuring cups, it was sometimes difficult to get the dish right and we had to go back and forth several times. She was always willing to help and clarify my doubts. Thank you, Ma!

Thank you, Avyan, my little fella, my biggest helper, for showing all your enthusiasm and love for Mumma's cooking! I hope this book will play some part in learning about the food and flavors that your Mumma grew up eating.

Thank you, Baba, Siddharth (my brother), Parmita (my sister-in-law), Mummy (my mother-in-law), Papa (my father-in-law), Archna (my sister-in-law) and Partha (my brother-in-law) for having tremendous faith in me and believing in my work.

A special thanks to my editor, Marissa Giambelluca, and my designer, Rosie Gutmann, for answering numerous questions and helping me make this book look just the way I wished it would. Thank you to the entire gang at Page Street for giving me this opportunity.

I am lucky to have some amazing friends in my life. Prerna and Vijitha, I can never thank you both enough for lending me your props, for testing my recipes, for believing in me, for being there with me at every step of this journey. Thank you Samiksha, Shruti, Deepa, Priya, Gaurav, Romita, Jenna, Jasmine, Anwesha, Noborupom, Subhajeet, Sukanya, Savita and Jhumi for motivating me, helping me with ideas and testing my recipes. Thank you Asha and Alanna for answering all my doubts.

And most importantly, thanks to the readers of Playful Cooking. Without you, this cookbook would have never existed. I hope you show this book the same love that you have showered me with on my blog.

About the Author

Kankana Saxena is a self-taught food photographer, food stylist and recipe developer. Originally from India, she is currently living in California with her husband and son. Her love for food started at a much later stage in life, which then led to her blog, Playful Cooking. The blog features a balanced mix of savory and sweet. It's mostly nutritional with a little bit of indulgence here and there. Her blog has been featured on several websites, including Saveur, HuffPost Taste, BuzzFeed Food, The Kitchn and eHow. She collaborates with different food brands to create recipes and photograph their products.

Kankana's blog covers a mix of cuisines from all around the world, but her native Bengali cuisine has always been close to her heart. Through this book, she shares various Bengali dishes, from street food to daily meals and from the most popular to some long-lost dishes, and hopes to reveal the vibrant and unique Bengali cuisine that she loves.

Index